halfway to CRazy

Mark Thrice

Morgan James Publishing • NEW YORK

halfway to crazy

Copyright ©2007 Mark Thrice

ISBN: 1-60037-012-8 (Paperback)

Published by:

MORGAN · JAMES
THE ENTREPRENEURIAL PUBLISHER™
www.morganjamespublishing.com

Cover/Interior Design by:

Rachel Campbell
rcampbell77@cox.net

Morgan James Publishing, LLC
1225 Franklin Ave Ste 32
Garden City, NY 11530-1693
Toll Free 800-485-4943
www.MorganJamesPublishing.com

Habitat
for Humanity®
Peninsula
Building Partner

DEDICATIONS

this book is dedicated to my fans and/or readers who keep me going with their ridiculous stories and warm encouragement.

Mostly though, it's dedicated to my awesome family: Steph, Duncan, Emma and Benjamin. Without you, I would have ABSOLUTELY nothing to write about, and how boring is that?

ACKNOWLEDGEMENTS

the line between 'acknowledgement' and 'blame' is a fine one. Depending on whether the guy in question is 'famous' or 'infamous', you may find yourself answering Oprah's questions regarding how well you mentored someone, or answering the reporter's questions regarding why your name is being used in reference to a disturbing psychological phenomenon.

Either way, you get on TV!

I want to make sure that I give an especially hard guy-type slap on the back to Mom and Dad, Linda and Rudy, Tess, Todd and Greg.

I also want to thank everyone that sent me stories and let me change the words just enough for me to make money off of them.

Finally, I want to thank Gayle Nichol and Dave Paul, two of the best editors a guy could have.

CONTENTS

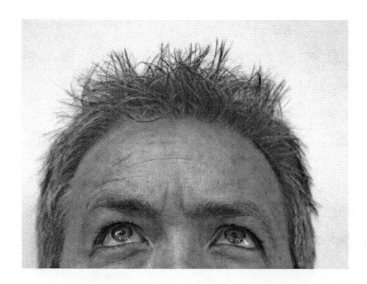

The Nine Steps

Man, as a species, has been hunted for centuries. If it were not for his faulty brain and the fact that he was attracted to his predators, he would have developed some sort of useful defence mechanism by now, like quills or huge, lobster-like claws. Instead, he has worked on his ability to emit a slightly poisonous gas and the power to neglect his own hygiene. This is not always the most effective arsenal to have. Some hunters are prepared to do whatever it takes to bag their game, even if it means liberal applications of cotton wads up the nose.

As ruthless as females are, I maintain that man's worst enemy is his own non-functioning brain. If a man's head was working properly, he would be safe no matter what a woman threw his way. As it is, she can talk him into pretty much ANYTHING. This is because a man becomes quite cooperative when his brain convinces him he'll be getting smooches in the near future. We all know how faulty this logic is, but the fact remains

2

that men ARE STILL BEING CAUGHT and domesticated in the same way they were hundreds of years ago.

How does this happen, you ask? It is an intricate process, perfected over the centuries by our rivals, the women. These may seem like innocent steps to the untrained bachelor's eye, but beware. They lead to heartache.

STEP ONE: Going Steady- Hurray for you, you got the girl. Keep your head up and your eyes open at all times or the next thing you know you'll be…

Gainfully Employed (STEP TWO) – What attractive woman wants to be associated with an unemployed bum? And how can you afford to give her the things she deserves (fancy meals, jewellery, etc.) unless you have some form of reliable cash flow. A talented guy like you should be able to do anything he wants to (except, of course, remain unemployed). Forget hanging out with your friends until all hours of the morning. Forget staying home to watch the back-to-back Seinfeld episodes starting at four each day. You've got something to prove! Go get 'em, champ! And while you're at it, don't forget to...

Change The Hairstyle (STEP THREE) – Probably the thing that attracted your mate to you was your long, rocker-style hair. Now that you have a job, isn't it time that you cut it off? How else will you get a promotion?

Obviously, your girl has a plan. Since your cool locks attracted HER, chances are that they will continue to attract females (you can't just turn something like that off). Now that you have been captured, you must be identified as "off the market." In biological circles, we call this being tagged.

STEP FOUR -Buying and wearing neckties- Accessories are necessary when one wants to make a fashion statement. Usually, a necktie says: "Doofus." The necktie's only function is to make you realize how desperately you need someone to help you match clothes before you leave the house for the job you just got. How fortunate that you happen to know someone who is willing to perform this function every day of your life.

STEP FIVE -Getting Married- I happen to love the institution of marriage. Having said that, I must admit that when my friend Stoobie told me HE was getting married, my response was, "Why?" In fact, that's what EVERY MARRIED MALE SAID TO HIM. Single guys don't realize that going from bachelorhood to couplehood is like going from golf to baseball: the importance of 'swinging' is replaced by the need to just 'head home.'

STEP SIX -Bedspreads- "WE'RE SPENDING HOW MUCH ON BLANKETS?? WELL, NOBODY ELSE SHOULD BE IN OUR BEDROOM!! I DON'T EVEN KNOW WHY WE BOTHER TO MAKE THE BED. WE'RE JUST GOING TO MESS IT UP IN A FEW HOURS ANYWAYS!! I CAN'T BELIEVE THAT A PORTION OF MY SALARY IS GOING TOWARDS SOMETHING CALLED A 'SHAM'!"

4

STEP SEVEN –Cleaning Out Your Drawers– Somehow, your new wife will get the idea that in order to make more space for the blanket accessories she just purchased, she must get rid of all of your old clothes. Now, granted, some of your clothes ARE pretty ragged. You may, in fact, have underwear that is held together by no more than a handful of underwear molecules. You may have concert t-shirts that don't fit you and haven't since cassettes were all the rage. HOWEVER, they are souvenirs that remind you of how much of a stud you once were. Prepare to lose them all.

STEP EIGHT –Having Kids–There is no part of a man's life that so aptly contrasts his former greatness to his present situation than the raising of a family. Childbirth, potty training, stomach flu… they all help to wipe away whatever remainder of coolth he had been saving. The icing on the cake is hating Barney, realizing that you know most of his songs and hating yourself.

STEP NINE –Getting Fixed– As soon as your wife decides that you are both done having kids, your last vestige of 'guyness' will be threatened. Discussion is futile.

You: "Honey, why don't YOU get fixed. It's easier."

Her: "I don't think so. Besides, I've done my 'hospital time' by bringing YOUR three children into this world."

You: "So you're used to being in the hospital. In fact, I bet you're a pro!"

Her: "Nice try. How about this: you don't touch me until the doctor 'touches' you."

You: "Don't make me choose between my two best friends."

Her: "See you when you get back!"

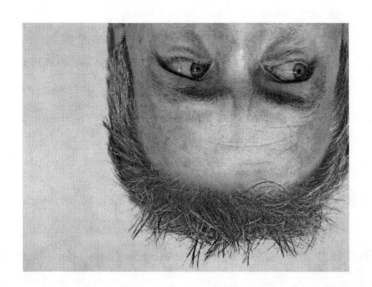

In The End, It's Just A Little Nip N Tuck

a vasectomy is to a group of men what childbirth is to a group of women: a shared crisis which brings them together. Of course, when you're young (and stupid) you don't think that kind of thing will ever concern you. After all, you are a man. If someone that you are married to wants to protect herself from getting pregnant, then she can just go get herself fixed. However, once one is married, one starts hearing the whispers of reality. Older husbands that you know and respect are overheard talking about "making the appointment." Senior staff members disappear from work for days at a time, only to return with a strange new love for frozen vegetables. This is nature's way of arousing a man's curiosity and, at the same time, preparing him for what must inevitably befall his person, as it were.

8

In many ways, I'm lucky that my wife knows me like the back of her hand. In fact, the back of her hand and I are well acquainted. Unfortunately, in this instance that relationship did not work to my advantage. In fact, I believe that I may have been downright manipulated into something that I'm not sure I wanted to do.

For the past year or so, we were debating as to whether we were done having kids. Husbands and wives use different data for making that decision. Husbands ask themselves questions like: "Do I feel like changing more diapers?", "When will I get to sleep through the night?" and "How soon can we kick the kids out so that my wife and I can get frisky?" Wives, on the other hand, are not rational at all. They do things like watch home movies; memorize Long Distance commercials and buy Anne Geddes calendars. These things should not be the basis for making life (and body) altering decisions.

As you know, the debate was put to rest when my wife got herself pregnant. Actually, being pregnant really did bring us to a resolution: "AAUGH! My legs! My back! This is DEFINITELY the last one!"

Having finally made a decision, I could breathe a sigh of relief. That is, until I discovered the exact consequences of that decision: "You need to make an appointment with the doctor. It's time."

Now let me just warn you guys that once a woman makes up her mind in this regard, nothing you can say will change it. In fact, the more you try to reason with her, the tougher she gets.

YOU: "Honey, I'm not sure this is a good idea."

HER: "Oh, it's a good idea alright. If you think that I'm going to push THREE children out of me AND THEN go in to get fixed, you've got another think coming!"

From this point, the conversation degrades into a long and descriptive diatribe of each child's delivery. To avoid getting nauseous, you make the stupid appointment. Even so, you are apprehensive of the course of action you seem to be on. Your mind is racing for a scheme that will get you out of this predicament. However, your wife KNOWS you and how your little brain works. No amount of thinking on your part could prepare you for the next day WHEN YOUR WIFE CHANGES HER MIND.

HER: "Honey, maybe you were right. Maybe we should wait. This baby is sooo cute. I would hate for it to be the last one..."

YOU: "WHAT?! You want MORE? No way! I'm getting fixed!"

And with that, you have suddenly sealed the deal. Perhaps when they are "fixing" you, they can do something about that faulty brain of yours, as well.

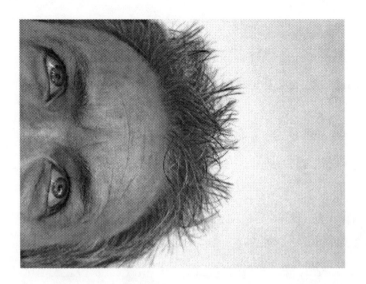

Tales From The Crypt
Of The Snipped

a man's worst enemy, besides his own faulty brain, is the male sense of humor. It represents THE OTHER voice in his head that he should most always ignore, but never does. A good example of this is his tendency to rib her about her cooking while her in-laws are over for dinner. Another is the concept of 'streaking'.

The worst (and best) of a guy's sense of humor becomes apparent when discussing the process of Getting Fixed. There has never been a clearer separation of groups within the male species: Those Who Are Snipped and Those Who Will Be.

Those Who Are Snipped have the definite advantage. They are older, wiser and more experienced. They have been through everything, will tell you anything and care nothing. There is nothing more fun to a "Snipped" person (or capon) than to regale his Unsnipped audience with stories of

12

surgeries past, full of metaphors involving ordinary household objects like tennis balls, bowling balls and grapefruit. And believe me, every "steer" has a story.

My buddy Corey's advice was to pick your surgeon carefully. Make an error here and you gain an intimate perspective on the aforementioned household objects.

On the other hand, my buddy R.W. advised me to stock up on certain medical supplies beforehand: "You need four or five bags of frozen peas. Not broccoli, not carrots. Peas. Specifically Green Giant brand. And tighty-whiteys. And track pants. You need a mixture of coolness, tightness and looseness. And don't plan on leaving the couch for at least three days." "I understand the need for special clothing," I said," but are the frozen peas THAT necessary?" He nodded vigorously. "They saved my life! I still can't look at the Green Giant without feeling warm in my heart and sick to my stomach."

If the horror stories are too effective, that may scare you away. The "Snipped" do not want this. As fun as it is to frighten you, the uninitiated, they still want you to go through with the operation. This reinforces the old axiom: "Misery loves company." It's kind of like a dog saying to his friends: "The leash" LOVE IT! It's really the best thing that ever happened to me. You should try one. It would look great on you!"

When my buddy Rob was thinking about having it done, he consulted with a friend of his. "It's no big deal!" his friend assured him. "In fact, I mowed my lawn the next day and I've got a five acre lot." After the operation, as Rob was lying in the fetal position on the couch, he phoned his friend again.

Rob: "Hey, I just want to say that I really respect you. I just got snipped and I'm dying here. I can't believe that you could mow your entire lawn after this operation."

Friend: "Oh that. I was just pulling your leg. Five acres of lawn would have killed me. Ha ha ha!"

Rob: "I think two "acres" will be the death of me."

So far, this should seem like a bad idea. Unfortunately, my brain is telling me that if THEY can do it, I can do it. And it probably won't even hurt me. To get a knowledgeable opinion that I can trust (since I can't really trust my friends OR my own brain), I decided to pay a visit to my old friend, Dr. Joe.

Me: "So, what can you tell me about Getting Snipped?"

Dr. Joe: "What? Vasectomies? There's nothing to it."

Me: "What do you mean, 'nothing'?"

Dr. Joe: "Well, it's a simple procedure. A small incision. A few cuts and you're done. Ha ha!"

Me: "What do you mean: 'done'?"

Dr. Joe: "Do you want me to make you an appointment?"

Me: "Do you know the doctor personally? On a first-name basis? Did he take care of you?"

14

Dr. Joe: "Oh, I myself haven't had it done."

Me: "WHAT??? YOU haven't had it done? Well, I'M sure not getting it done."

My Wife: "Whoa there, big boy. Let's all just take a deep breath and settle down. You've already said that you would."

Me: "I curse my faulty brain."

My Wife: "It's not your brain that's the trouble here."

All the way home, I tried my darndest to use Dr. Joe as a reason to renege on my promise.

Me: "But dear, if a medical professional doesn't do it, it bears looking into. Doesn't it make you a wee bit paranoid? Kind of like a cook who refuses to eat his own soup."

My Wife: "Maybe he's Catholic..."

Me: "How come they get off so easily? I wonder if they're accepting new members...."

As it is, if I don't convert I'll go through with it. I swear, though, that when it's MY turn to explain the whole procedure to some terrified schmuck, I won't take advantage of him.

Unless it's really, really funny.

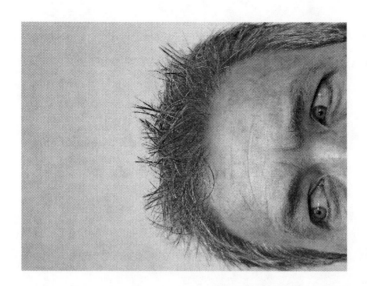

The Deed Is Done

there are many sources out there who will tell you this and that. Know that you can count on me and my journal to give you the straight up on how the whole Surgical Procedure goes "down."

I have to say that I wasn't really nervous about going to the hospital. It didn't bother me to think about having an operation, even an operation "down there." I must confess, though, that for the preceding few days, the STRANGEST thoughts ran through my head: what if my wife loses all interest in me, now that I have been truly 'domesticated'; what if the Red Chinese take over and have no use for 'men' who cannot produce slaves for their evil purposes; what if I develop 'Man Breasts?'

My appointment was set for 10:30 am. The trip to the hospital was full of instruction for post-op care.

Me: "So after you drop me off, what are you going to do?"

16

My Wife: "(sigh) Buy three bags of Green Giant frozen peas."

Me: "And?"

My Wife: "Go to the video store and rent six DVD's for you. Honestly honey, do you really think you are going to have time to watch SIX movies?"

Me: "I'd better have."

As soon as I was dropped off, everything went like clockwork.

10:30 -Saunter into the hospital as cool as a cucumber, as it were. Look for the admitting desk.

10:32 -Find an elderly volunteer. "Can I help you?" she asks. "Yes, I'm here for a vasectomy." I reply. She gets flustered and runs away. "That was fun," I think to myself. I decide that if the opportunity presents itself, I'll find another volunteer and do it again.

10:37 -The nurse in admitting takes my 'information.' "I'm here to see Dr. John. We don't have to discuss why." "Oh, I know why you're here," she says. "Now you'll see what we women have to go through every time we have a baby."

10:50 -Along with my nifty new bracelet, I hurry off in search of the Day Surgery Ward, which is simply "straight ahead, veer left, down the ramp, through the doors and on the fifth floor..." A voice inside tells me that now would be a good time to run. I wonder if cattle feel a real sense of purpose as they await their turn to meet Oscar Meyer.

11:00 - "WELCOME TO DAY SURGERY!" A nurse gives me some little blue pills, then takes my blood pressure, height, weight, pulse and next of kin.

Me: "Why do you need THAT?"

Nurse Lynn: "Oh, ha ha! Just a formality! By the way, is everything shaved?"

Me: "Yes. I did a wonderful job. You don't need to check. I have to tell you, though, it's making me VERY uncomfortable."

Nurse Lynn: "Well, now you know what women go through when they shave their bikini line for you."

Me: "For the record, I've never requested that."

11:07 - Spend ten minutes trying to tie my gown behind my back. Pray I am not on Candid Camera.

11:17 - I lay in bed, idly wondering important things like what was in those little blue pills, where the sun comes from and whether or not trees dream.

11:30 - I awaken in the operating room. I feel it necessary to introduce myself to all twelve nurses looking at my undercarriage.

Dr. John: "What did you do to your legs?"

Me: "Well, I had a little time on my hands and drew some arrows, in case you got lost. By the way, who's got the munchies?"

18

11:40 -Pin prick. Pin prick.

12:03 -*Dr John:* "Well, that's it. We're done."

Me: "That didn't take long. Did you get both sides?"

Dr John: "Yes, we got both sides. Take it easy for a few days. You'll be fine."

2:00 -Wake up and find my wife by my side. Get dressed and fill my pants with ice. Leave the hospital in true cowboy style: Bow-legged!

3:00 -Celebrate V-Day by sleeping, watching movies and falling in love with frozen vegetables. Make plans for a better party to commemorate this day, next year.

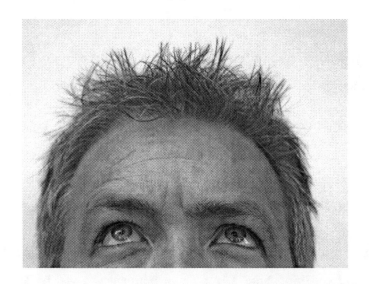

"Home Free" After A Delicate Procedure

being "home-free" is one of the best feelings in the world, whether you are playing tag or recovering from an important "procedure" done on an important "area." Being home-free means that you are safe from such announcements as, "You're it!" or "Guess what! "Yes, I am happy to say that in the Family Game, I am Home-Free. Since I am still getting e-mails from potential candidates and their wives ("Can you please tell him that it's going to be okay?"), I will let you in on What To Expect When You Know She Won't Be Expecting.

#1 You have just shaved everything from your waist down to your ankles. Be prepared to be itchy. This is why they put those big cone things on dogs after they're fixed. Oh, to be as flexible as Lucky! Decide now to either not scratch at all or stay in the basement for the next two weeks.

20

#2 Your wife will adopt one of those, "I Hope You Understand What Women Go Through When They Shave" attitudes. Like THAT helps.

#3 Talcum powder will be your best, best friend in the whole world and you will never forget the great service that it did for you. AAAH, SOOOOTHING!

#4 The same guys you talked to BEFORE the surgery, the ones who made reference to all sorts of large citrus fruit, will change their story afterwards and say things like, "Aren't you better yet? I was back to work in two days!" May they find their stockings full of Reindeer Clumps this December.

#5 Finally, the test. After every major event in life, there's a test. There's your driver's test when you're sixteen; exams in university; your marriage test (every time your wife says something like, "Tell me why you love me.") Coincidentally, there is also a test of sorts for this most important surgery of your life. Using my previous "Little Soldiers Analogy," you need to make sure that the "barracks" are sealed and the camp is deserted. To pass THIS test, you are given a sterile cup....

Once you have completed your test; you have two hours to rush your "results" to the hospital, find the lab and drop them off. But before you go off half-cocked, waving your sample around at every available nurse, you may want to think about what you are doing. I'm sure the big joke in the hospital is watching The Parade of Nervous Guys Who Are Trying To Conceal Their Tupperware. My recommendation is to put the sample into something inconspicuous like a Happy Meal Bag. Everyone loves a Happy Meal!

Following that comes the worst part of the whole procedure. Worse than the swelling, the discomfort or the lack of sympathy is waiting for the results. Traditionally, the lab will tell you not to call them but to contact your doctor after about a week. And, traditionally, when you call him, his receptionist will tell you that he is gone for the rest of the summer! HAHAHA! A little urology humour there!

The Doctor: "Mark, you passed your test. Good work!"

Me: "I gave it all I had. Thanks for the 'Home-Free' pass, Doc!"

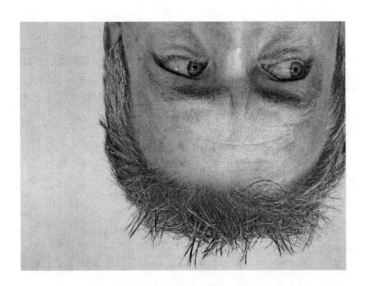

The Little Engine That Wanted Some Friends... For $14.95

t homas the Tank Engine™ was sad. "What's the matter, Thomas™?" asked Mavis, the Big Black Diesel Engine™.

"I'm bored," said Thomas™, "bored and lonely."

"Let's go for a ride!" said Mavis™. She had newly arrived over the Christmas holidays and was quite content to run along the Figure Eight Track™ all day long.

"No, I don't want to." said Thomas™ sourly. "And besides, there's no one to play with."

"What about all of your new friends: Duncan and Annie and Clarabelle and the NW Brake Van? Each valued at $14.95?"

"Know who I wish was here?" lamented Thomas™, who was now absent-mindedly picking his nose.

24

"Who?" asked Mavis™, who suppressed the urge to call him an unthankful little weasel.

"Gordon™ and Henry™. They are my favorites."

"What about Percy™ and Oliver™?" asked Mavis™.

"Yes, they're my favorites too."

"And James™?"

"Yes, James™ is my favorite too. I wish I had James™ here."

"But didn't you just go to the toy store YESTERDAY and pick out Duncan, the Grumpy Scottish Steam Engine™? I think there's a lesson we need to remind ourselves of.", said Mavis™ wisely, and patiently.

"The refund policy at the toy store?"

"No. Not the refund policy at the toy store. The lesson I'm thijnking about is that Really Useful Engines™ are always THANKFUL."

"Yeah," said Thomas™, "James™ is a really useful engine. I wish I had James™."

"You know, " reminded Mavis™, in a slightly louder train-voice, "another thing we could be thankful for is your genuine Clickety-Clack Track™. If we had got a track last year, it wouldn't have Clickety-Clacked™. That would have been 80 bucks down the old boiler."

Just then Duncan, the Grumpy Scottish Steam Engine™ chugged into the station.

"Where in the name of Fergus McBuffer is an engine to get a wee bit o' shut eye?" he asked.

"What do you mean?" asked Thomas, the Really Ungrateful Engine™.

"The RRRound house™ lady!" exclaimed Duncan™ rolling his r's in traditional Scottish™ fashion, "Where's the RRRound house™ where all the steam engines™ sleep after a hard day of work, as seen on all six "Thomas and Friends™" videos?"

"Don't have one." sighed Thomas™.

"Don't start," warned Mavis™, who was wondering how much the wooden trains would be appreciated as they made their way to the living room fireplace.

"Don't have one?" yelled Duncan™. "I see I'm not the only one with Scottish blood in me. They're only $144.95! Hey Annie™, Clarabelle™! C'mere lassies! Did ye know there's no RRRound house™?"

"No guff," said Annie™.

"We've been here two months and not one set has been added!" said Clarabelle™.

"Not the Freight Yard Expansion Pack™®?" asked the Scottish Troublemaker™.

"Nope."

"What about the 'James Goes Buzz Buzz' Set™ or the Percy Takes the Plunge Story Set™?"

"Nope. We don't even have the Lifting Bridge© or Henry's™ Tunnel® from the Classic Video™® 'Come Out Henry™'", whined Thomas™ as he looked for something to wipe his finger on.

"Bust my buffers!" said Duncan™.

"Don't tempt me," said Mavis™. "Maybe you™®© and Clarabelle™ need to spend some time in the Spooky Tunnel that doubles as the Cold Air Return Duct."

26

When all the Engines™ realized that Mavis™ wasn't just "blowing steam" it was much easier to enjoy each other's company AND the little Figure Eight Track™. And everyone was Happy.

(At least for another day.)

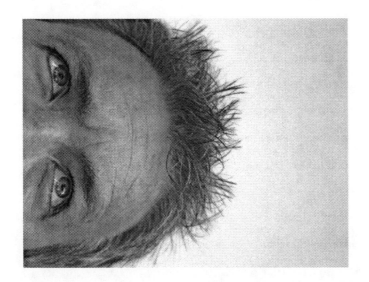

A Fine Kettle

When it comes to the Art of Shopping, my mother is a Master. Being retired, she can afford to spend her days cruising the city with her friends, looking for deals and, well, I guess looking for more deals. I don't know if I'm real PROUD to say this or not but most of her purchases come from a store by the name of Value Village.

For those of you who are not in the "know" or possibly in the "care," Value Village is a store that resells previously enjoyed merchandise. It is a veritable treasure-trove of...um...merchandise that has been enjoyed previously. There are, according to the experts (my mother), many great bargains to be had there. This fact, for her, would be like a flame to your common moth. Some days, she gets more than she planned.

Last weekend, she and a friend paid their weekly visit. They split up and went their separate ways. Mom ended up in the "home decor" section

28

and found a beautiful tea kettle. It was large and very new-looking with blue enamel on the outside and white enamel on the inside. "This is a great deal," she thought to herself. That is the way her brain warns her wallet that it is about to be called upon. But don't think that my mother is the type of person who would just go into a store, find something that catches her eye and buy it on a whim.

Heavens! Don't think that.

Before buying anything, my mother subjects her prospective purchases to a rigid inspection process that leaves no question as to the quality of the item in-hand. For example, with clothing, you tug on all the seams. With toys, you check for choking hazards, cracks and loose parts. With tea kettles, you check the inside of the spout for chips.

Why? I don't know. I'm sure there must be a good reason. Much like there must be a good reason for the WAY in which you perform this check: you jam your pointer finger down as far as it will go.

The ordinary, run-of-the-mill consumer may experience a small problem retrieving her finger from the aforementioned spout. Rest assured, my mom is far beyond ordinary.

Yes, it's true. As soon as it went in, it was solidly glued to the inside of that kettle. And there she stood in all of her glory, purse in one hand and kettle stuck; spout first, on Peter Pointer.

The other shoppers began to stare.

Mom was not worried. "All I have to do is add a little moisture and my finger will slip right out," she reasoned. Casually, she lifted her finger up to her mouth and began licking her finger AND the spout all the way around.

The other shoppers began to step away.

Realizing that she was making a scene, she turned, nonchalantly tucked the kettle into her armpit, bent her head down and began licking in earnest. Finger, Thumb, Spout, Handle...if it was within reach, it was getting moisturized.

The other shoppers were suddenly VERY interested in their purchases.

Mom didn't notice because she was locked in a life or death struggle with a second-hand kitchen appliance. In her eyes, she was making great headway, but to everyone else, she was digging for chiggers.

Finally, and not a moment too soon, the kettle relented and released her finger: POP!

Everyone breathed a sigh of relief.

A few minutes later, my mom's friend appeared.

My Mom: "Where were you? I got a kettle stuck on my finger and had to lick it until it came off. I'm keeping it, though. I can tell it's a good deal. I'm a Master Shopper!"

Her Friend: "You're certainly a piece of work!"

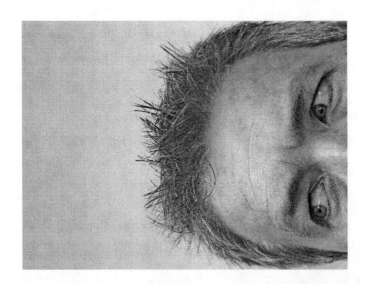

Yippee... a Chivaree!

It can't really be said that my older sister Teresa and I got along well for most of our childhood. In fact, it is a testament to the mysterious ways of Providence that we both reached adulthood unscathed. Whatever it was that kept us at odds during our formative years disappeared when I moved out of the house to go to university. That fact in itself could be an indicator of where the trouble lay.

Upon my return from school, we started to get along quite famously, she and I. In fact, I was even honoured with the Master of Ceremonies duties at her wedding. This involved entertaining everyone during the reception, keeping the program running smoothly and bringing the gifts back to her townhouse when all was said and done.

"Kim, my bridesmaid, will let you in." she explained, figuring that Kim would stick around to supervise.

32

I will now state this in print as an absolute truth. The events that transpired next were KIM'S IDEA. Not mine, as has been previously believed. Kim is the devil.

"Hmm." she said. "Someone could really do a great CHIVAREE in here and no one would know for at least a week."

This got me to thinking.

"What's a chivaree?" I thought. Then I remembered stories from Watford involving visits paid to the homes of newlywed couples where labels were ripped off of canned goods, toilet paper was flung about willy-nilly and the house was left with an ambience of chaos.

"I couldn't do that." I said. "At least, not without help."

One big difference between being a Man and being a Guy is that if you are a Guy, you have friends that you can count on, no matter what time of the day or night, no matter where you are, to help you toilet paper your sister's house.

"Greg," I said, "I'm in my sister's house and she won't be home for a week."

"I'll be right over." he replied.

As much as I hate to brag, I must say that the ensuing hour saw some of the most CREATIVE chivareeing in the history of the planet. Not only were all the labels removed from every can on the premises, we also managed to "think outside the box".

Did you know that if you place a so-called 'Cooking Onion' in the microwave and cook it for eighteen minutes IT DOES ABSOLUTELY NOTHING? It doesn't sizzle. It doesn't burn. It doesn't explode. But when you remove it, it weighs nothing at all. It seems that over-cooking a Cooking Onion somehow removes its soul.

I had actually forgotten about our mission until I got a phone call two weeks later.

"I'm bringing over a batch of butter tarts and you are going to eat every one of them."

Me: "Sure thing, sis. What's the problem?"

Her: "I'll tell you what the problem is. I was making a Roast Beef dinner tonight and was mixing the gravy on the stove and for some reason it EXPLODED..."

Me: "Uh, sounds like you got your baking soda and your corn starch mixed up. It could happen to any..."

Her: "...THEN I decide to mix some drinks for my guests and notice CHICKEN chunks in the lemon mix..."

Me: "Chicken soup stock actually, and I told Greg..."

Her: "...THEN I try a butter tart that I spent ALL DAY making and they BURN MY TONGUE!! What did you put in the corn syrup, Tabasco Sauce™? I just tried to calm my nerves with a cup of coffee but IT tastes like French Onion Soup!"

Me: "By any chance, did you heat it up in the microwave?"

Her: Click

34

People often ask me how I ended up marrying such a NICE girl. I can honestly state that my choice for a wife reflected not only how much I loved her but also how much everyone else loved her, and would REALLY hate to ruin her kitchen.

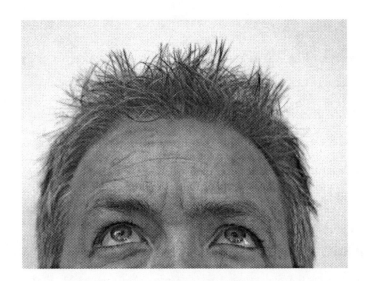

A Nair-ow Miss

men have problems on a lot of fronts, mostly because of the women in their lives. They start their lives being reminded to clean their rooms and change their underwear. Then, as they enter adolescence, they are played against each other for sport. Finally, years later, they bring their bride into their castle, their homestead and slowly watch it become 'cute.'

I don't know what exactly a wife does to make a man feel like a stranger in his own home. I can tell you that nothing throws a guy's balance off more than "doilies." What ARE these things? What are they good for? In one day, a bunch of frilly, lace Frisbees can turn a comfortable pad into a Living Area. And that, my friends, is the last time you have ANY of your friends over.

36

I think that women like to keep men on their toes. Maybe they think that we're too cocky. Maybe they just really don't like us. But they keep coming up with things like: "Don't wear white after Labour Day," Tupperware parties, fruit nappies and those little tiny coffee tables that you're not allowed to put anything on. And for the most part, we don't notice until it actually starts to affect us.

Take, for example, my friend Ron. Ron had a really bad experience IN HIS OWN HOME because of something that his wife Kathy decided to change. She did not tell him about this change. She just MADE the change and waited for him to notice.

The other day, Ron decided to take their son Matthew down to the docks to go fishing. Ron knew that it was a sunny day and therefore the rays reflecting off of the water could give him sunburn. So he told Kathy that he was going to put some sunscreen on. Now, at this point in the story, the Guy Readers are thinking: "Way to use the old noggin, Ron! Thinkin' ahead improves your chances of getting some lovin' tonight!" By contrast, the Female Readers are thinking: "What about the boy? Did he even think to get sunscreen for the boy?" The answer is: "Probably not." But that is not the point of my story, so all of you Female Readers can go make doilies somewhere and stop interrupting a guy here!!

Anyway, Ron headed to the bathroom and grabbed the sun block from its place on the shelf. He gave himself a liberal application on all of his exposed skin and PUT THE CONTAINER BACK WHERE IT BELONGED. He then proceeded to start loading the van with the fishing gear.

As he walked past Kathy, she noticed a familiar fragrance. What WAS that hanging in the air? (Wives find themselves asking that a lot in the first few years of marriage.) (Then they stop.) She recognized the smell as being associated with something unpleasant but couldn't quite put her finger on it. At the same time, Ron had finished loading the gear and was getting into the van. Kathy's scream suddenly rang throughout the house: "RON! RON! GET OUT OF THE VAN!"

Of course, Ron reacted like any young man with instant reflexes and nerves of steel: "Huh?"

Kathy: "GET OUT OF THE VAN! YOU HAVE TO JUMP IN THE SHOWER!"

Ron: "What??"

Kathy (opening the door of the van and pulling Ron out onto the driveway): "GET IN THE SHOWER QUICK! GO GO GO GO GO!"

Ron: "What has gotten into you?"

Kathy: "YOU JUST COVERED YOUR BODY WITH NAIR AND YOU HAVE TO WASH IT OFF BEFORE IT STARTS TO WORK!"

Ron: "AAAAAAAAUUUUUGH!"

Yes, it was true. For some reason known only to Kathy, the parking spot for Ron's sunscreen, the spot that had belonged to the sunscreen since the dawn of mankind (as far as Ron was concerned) had been taken over by the NAIR-MOBILE, the instant-hair-remover that women love and love to hate.

38

Kathy's point was deceptively simple: "All you have to do is read the labels."

Ron, however, also had a strong argument: "I shouldn't have to READ the labels when I know where everything belongs!"

And by the time his eyebrows grow back, he'll have found a new spot for his sun block.

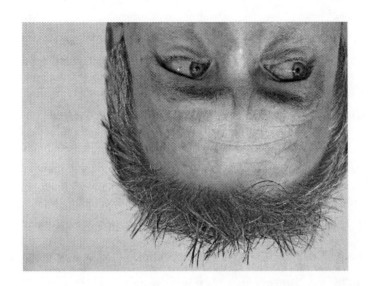

A Visit From Mr. Nose-Whistle

i have the solution to world peace. It's the same thing that will guarantee long, healthy lives and promote better relations between parents and kids: a good night's sleep. Why sleep is so elusive to ME is understandable. We have a baby. Now don't get me wrong, our baby "sleeps through the night." If you don't have kids yet, learn this phrase. It represents the Holy Grail of parenting.

The sun always shines on someone whose child "sleeps through the night." As parents, we often invoke this phrase while talking with other young parents, even though the boy could have been up eight times the night before. Everyone wants a child who "sleeps through the night" even if "the night" means from 2 a.m. to 4 a.m. Yep, that was the night and he slept right through it.

40

Anyway, even if your child actually DOES sleep until morning, you are always "on call." Sure, you fall asleep but your brain is still expecting to hear something so it doesn't let your body get sleeping TOO deeply. So when you can convince your brain that everything is OK (or that your wife will get up), you need to take advantage of your time and snooze.

Last Thursday was such a night. My wife wasn't working the next day, so I knew that she was "on call" for the baby. I climbed into bed and rolled around a couple of times to get comfortable. (I had a dog once that did the same. This was no surprise.) My wife snuggled close and laid her head on my arm. This basically meant that I had to get comfortable without moving anymore, because there was no moving her.

I started to relax and just as I was about to meet Mr. Sandman, I was assaulted by Mr. Nose-Whistle. I don't know if you have ever had the misfortune of meeting this dastardly villain, but he is my arch-nemesis. Instead of making your eyelids heavy, he makes your nose sound like a dime-store flute: small, irritating and unstoppable. You must understand how frustrating this can be.

The room is still and dark. As things get settled, our breathing grows deeper. Something is wrong, though. Instead of inhale/exhale, I hear Fwee-Fwee-Fwee-Fwee. Mr. Nose-Whistle has struck again. But, now the problem is that I can't move. If I could move, I could blow or pick or fill my passages with Vap-O-Rub, but I can't. So I whistle. And whistle.

My wife wakes up and asks me if I'm calling the dog. We don't have a dog. I bury my head in the pillow and this stifles the noise. However, it also reduces the oxygen to my brain. Sensing danger, I turn my face and press my nose against her ear. Now we've gone from whistle to French Horn and my wife thinks I'm goofing around. (Me?)

Now I've got to become a mouth-breather in order for BOTH of us to get to sleep. Luckily, even Mr. Nose-Whistle gets tired and I finally get some shut-eye, none the worse for wear. Even as I doze, I contemplate the value (or possibility) of shaving one's nasal passage.

Hmmmm.

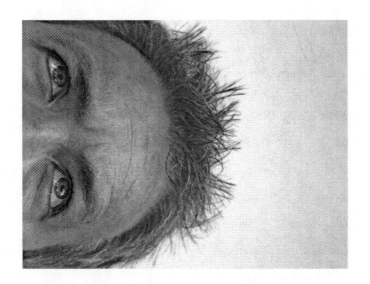

Avoiding
Household Dangers

danger lurks in the Thrice household. As far as my kids are concerned, that danger is in the form of hornets. They (the kids) see them (the hornets) as everything that is evil in this world: angry, flesh-devouring insects that single you out on a whim and chase you down until you are dead.

In my opinion, household danger is represented by marbles. That's right. Marbles. Little round glass hellions that are invisible to the eye and magnetically attracted to the soles of your feet. When they operate independently, they are painful nuisances. As a group, they are a lethal force to be reckoned with. And they're everywhere. In the kitchen, in the living room, in the bedroom, waiting, watching, breeding, taunting you

44

with every 'click' and 'clack', finding their way under your feet. Oh, the horror...the horror...

The most dangerous thing in my wife's world, however, is food. I did not know this when we were dating. In fact, I don't even know how I would have posed it as a question. (How do you feel about leftover bologna?) I'm not saying that it would have made a big difference to me. I'm just saying that Forewarned is Forearmed.

It all started when our children were little. Food posed a choking hazard. To a certain extent, I agreed with her. It was important to watch our kids as they ate and to make sure that what they were eating wouldn't block their tiny little airways. That's why my policy was to avoid sharing any of my food with them, if at all possible. (Now that they are older, my policy is to cover my food with a layer or two of Jalapeno peppers.)

Her fears went beyond the traditional 'mouthful of chicken,' though. In my wife's eyes, choking dangers lurked everywhere, from JELLO to hot chocolate powder to dust mites and shower caps.

Our big problem now that they are older is trying to safeguard ourselves from Things That Rot Quickly. (All of you unmarried guys out there PLEASE pay attention. This concerns subject matter that you HAVE to know about your future spouse.) In a way, I feel naive. First about the fact that I had no idea how quickly food can turn from tasty morsel to LETHAL MOUTHFUL OF DEATH. Secondly about the fact that the woman I married is a loon. In her eyes, it is better to err on the side of caution. In my eyes, it is better to NOT throw the milk out just because it sat in the van for a few hours before you got home. No, in our household, no one will ever die of salmonella poisoning. We would, in fact, starve first.

Me: "Honey, where's the lunch meat?"

My Wife: "It was starting to smell funny so I threw it out."

Me: "But I just pulled it out of the fridge for lunch."

My Wife: "And you set it directly in the SUNLIGHT. Blecch! Who knows what's growing on it now?"

Me: "Well, certainly not me..."

My Wife: "By the way, we need another bag of milk and a new jar of mayonnaise."

Me: "Let me guess...our friend Mr. Sun?"

My Wife: "I'm just trying to keep everyone healthy. By the way, I think that we should make another trip to the grocery store. I can't believe how fast we go through food..."

Me: "Suddenly I feel sick."

Everything my wife stands for directly contravenes what I learned as a bachelor. And let me preface what I'm about to say by mentioning that a little diarrhea is good for you. It cleans you out.

Living as a bachelor meant recycling. Yesterday's breakfast dishes became tonight's supper dishes. And there were times when, yes, yesterday's

46

breakfast became tonight's supper. My philosophy towards eating was that you could eat ANYTHING no matter what condition it was in. If you happened to chew something that tasted a little 'tangy,' you'd spit it out and move on to another spot. This was especially true for pizza which, after some crude experimentation, could still provide important nutrients even after a full week of sitting under the bed. Like democracy, this idea was born out of necessity. I had to eat SOMETHING and my money had already been frivolously spent on tuition and school books.

Our children will be spared these trials by the time they reach their college years. I have no doubt their mother will continue to protect them by setting up camp outside their refrigerator doors. This will leave me free to fend for myself and stash as much pizza under our bed as possible.

Baking 101

et me begin by saying this: the column that I wrote a few weeks ago about the fact that my generation doesn't bake elicited more than a few responses, some of them even printable in this family publication. Needless to say, the fact that I did get so many responses can only lead me to one conclusion: you people have too much time on your hands. I mean, really, you can't complain that you are "too busy" to bake when you obviously have time in your day to read, and reply to highly useless columns like my own. No, the simple truth is that when it comes to making "goodies", the Boomers have it and we don't. Which reminds me of that song from the rock band, THE WHO entitled "My Generation":

> *People try to put us down*
> *Just because our tarts turn brown*

48

Eat your cake before it gets c-c-cold

Don't blame me if it tastes like mold

X is my generation

It's my generation, baby

The oatmeal cookies taste like RAID

Can't dig my food without a sp-sp-spade

Whose pastries give your throat abrasions?

I'm talkin' 'bout my g-g-generation

X is my generation

It's my generation, baby

Of course, for every rule there is an exception. And in this case, her name is Amanda P. The email that she sent me fairly reeked of sugar and spice. "I take issue with your statement that our generation can't bake." she wrote. "Name the day and the time and I'll prove you wrong."

Being a Professional Journalist who is interested only in purveying the Truth, I sought out my editor because I had several issues that I had to wrestle with before I replied: **#1-** what if I invite her to the office and it turns out that I was wrong?

#2- worse still, what if I was right?

#3- worst of all, what if this starts a baking frenzy where suddenly our office is DELUGED with sweets from my fellow members of Generation X?

"Better call her right away." she said. "And Mark, there's no need to mention this little challenge to the rest of the editorial staff. Let's keep it professional."

And professional it was, from the way we professionally greeted Amanda before she actually entered the building to the way we, summoning every bit of Journalistic Integrity, professionally snorked down an entire OREO cookie cheesecake, followed by a plate of Chocolate Caramel Shortbread and a (small) batch of Fudge Brownies. AND LET ME SAY THIS: eating my words has never been so enjoyable (or calorie-filled).

So, officially, I retract my statement. Not EVERY member of my generation is baking-handicapped. To be fair, though, I've only seen proof of ONE exception. As far as I know, no one else in our demographic is any good at all when it comes to Oatmeal Chocolate Chip cookies or Strawberry Shortcake or even those little squares with the coconut, chocolate chips and condensed milk. Man, I'd sure hate to eat my words twice!

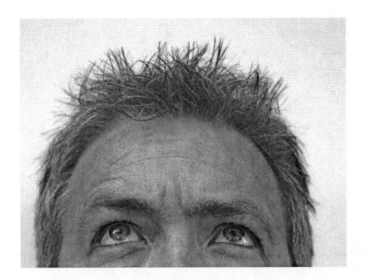

A Small Dose of Golf

nothing defines the summer months of the corporate world like watching the schedule fill up with golf tournaments. In fact, golf tournaments are the reason this country is in the sad state it is: nobody does any work after Thursday at 5:00 pm. Instead, all the leaders of the industry can be found on Fridays, adding pre-cancerous cells to their bodies in the middle of a field somewhere. This does not stop tournament organizers from trying to get more and more people out onto the course. Soon there will be no one left in the offices around the city to answer the phone and say that everyone is out playing golf. In fact, tournament organizers have become so desperate for players that they have even asked ME to be the "celebrity" golfer in one of their tournaments. The conversation went something like this:

Organizer: "Mr. Thrice, we're having a Celebrity Golf Tournament to raise money for charity."

52

Me: "So what."

Organizer: "Well, every threesome will pay big money to get to rub elbows with a celebrity for 18 holes of golf."

Me: "I GET BRITNEY SPEARS! STAMPED IT! NO CALLBACKS!"

Organizer: "Mr. Thrice, YOU would be the celebrity."

Me: "Me? What did I ever do to you?"

Organizer: "What do you mean?"

Me: "As much as I'd like to hang around a bunch of strangers for six hours in the hot sun, I think I'm much better in small doses."

Organizer: "Really?"

Me: "That's why my editor only prints my column once a week."

Organizer: "But your paper only comes out once a week."

Me: "Really??"

I effectively avoided any such commitment for quite a while until my editor Dave Paul decided to pick on me. "Thrice", he said, "it's time we made a man out of you." "HA!" I replied. "Good luck!"

I have to admit that a day of golf with my boss was a real eye opener. He introduced me to all the different elements of golf including the fescue, the bogey and bad pants. Under his patient tutelage, I learned different techniques and the common terms of the golfer. Most of them are not printable in this family-style newspaper. He also coached me in how to get the ball closer to the pin. He gave tips like:

"Keep looking, I think it landed further out", "Check over there in the long grass", "Throwing the ball is cheating" and "Try it from the women's tee. It landed there anyway."

We were entered in a tournament with a "shotgun" start. This means that they employ a shotgun to make sure one doesn't leave early. It also refers to the drinking game one plays when one is in the clubhouse afterwards and suffering from heatstroke.

We came very close to winning until the judges decided that it was the LOWEST score they were looking for. Then it wasn't even close. But that brought us to the best part of the "tourney": the prize table. It turns out that no matter how bad your golf coach is, if your team gets picked, you can run up to the table and go wild!

Me: "Boy, I could really get into this tournament thing."

Dave: "I think golfing with you is like working with you."

Me: "Why is that?"

Dave: "It really is best in small doses."

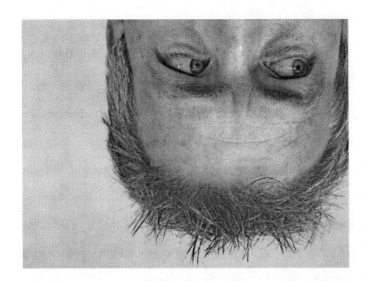

Camping Advice

When planning a camping trip, much time should be spent on preparation. This includes deciding how much food you need, what gear you are going to use and how many hair brushes to bring. You cannot be too careful about the latter point because, I mean really, even though you are fifty kilometres from the nearest town does not mean that you should give up on the basic tenets of personal hygiene and fashion. Other mandatory items include: make up, four different pairs of shoes and a trunk full of various items "for when the kids get bored" and, NO, you can't bring your hunting knife or anything else that would protect you from a bear if, God forbid, one should stumble onto your campsite and threaten your family in a menacing way (as opposed to threatening your family in a friendly way like, say, inviting them all over to an 'Amway for Bears' meeting).

56

As I was saying, you also need to decide on what food to bring. Make a list of all the healthy, natural types of snacks you can think of (nuts, fruit, baby carrots, broccoli, 'tofu'). These will be for your children. Now imagine yourself in Willy Wonka's Chocolate Factory. Everything that you see in your mind's eye is what you are allowed to buy for yourself. You do not need to worry about putting on any weight during your foray into the forest because of something called "Nature Mode": from the day you leave until the day you return, you will actually burn every calorie you ingest, so you might as well take advantage of it. For you sceptics, here is a handy chart that we "People In The Know" use quite frequently:

Packing equipment into van..................3000 calories

Driving for 6 hours with 2 hyper kids.......1500 calories

Setting up the tent.........................2000 calories

Slathering kids in bug repellent............1200 calories

Slathering kids in sun block (SPF 30).......1200 calories

Washing layers off of kids in shower........2500 calories

Getting kids to sleep in tent...............5000 calories

Getting campfire to light using wood you bought from a guy on the side of the road for FIVE DOLLARS AN ARMFULL.....9000 calories

Getting changed in tent while kids sleep....2500 calories

So there you have it. In one day, you have burned almost THIRTY THOUSAND calories! You are a mere shadow of your former self. Do you realize how many "Rosebuds" you will now have to eat just to keep up? Lots!

When it's time to pack your gear, you must remember that while camping, ANYTHING could happen. It is in your best interest to have a good variety of resources to fall back upon. This includes different sets of clothes for the different types of weather you may experience. It may get very cool; bring pants, sweatshirts and warm sleeping bags. It may rain; bring boots, raincoats and umbrellas. It may be terribly hot and humid; bring lots of bug repellent as you will probably be sleeping naked. (Know that this WILL NOT be appealing to your wife, even if you're using vanilla-scented DEET).

A final popular item with campers today is the "folding camping chair." This is a piece of furniture designed for maximum portability and minimum comfort, unless you already have an unnatural curve in your spine and no feeling in your legs. Plus, you get to burn an extra 4000 calories trying to get the stupid thing to open. If worse comes to worse, since you don't have any other weapons, you could use it as a club when the bears come to visit.

As I said earlier, when camping, much time should be spent in preparation. A well-prepared camper is one who has the correct gear, ample food and twelve pounds of "Rosebuds".

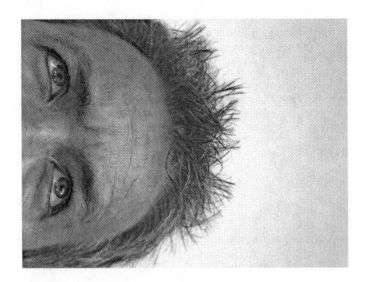

Christmas Traditions

a t this time of year, our attention turns to traditions of the season. One of the most exciting traditions that we celebrate in this part of the country is called "The Gift Game."

If you are tired of the mundane old routine of "Spending time thinking of what gift to buy for someone special, THEN searching high and low to find it," consider The Gift Game where you buy a present with NO ONE in mind! That's right! You just head right out to your favourite mall, plaza or house of worship and pick up anything of interest. By that I mean, of course, anything of interest to YOU. In fact, if you break this great tradition right down, it's all about hedging your bets for the holidays: if there is absolutely NOTHING of any value in the Gift Game for you, take your own gift back and the day won't be a total loss. This is the true meaning of Christmas.

60

The rules are as follows:

Rule #1: Agree on a Price Range. Usually everybody whines about how expensive Christmas is getting so you all agree to spend about ten bucks on each other. You then spend forty bucks in gas running from store to store trying to find something, ANYTHING that costs TEN DOLLARS! You will not, unless you are in the sock department at SEARS. Actually, you do have a few choices, including a fruitcake, a small box of TURTLES or a 'gag' gift such as: "Pull My Finger" a CD I received several years ago. (99 tracks of Flatulent Sound Effects. Includes the Hit: Yankee 'Doody' Dandy!) These are your limitations ONLY IF you are shopping RETAIL. There is a world of options open to you if you decide to broaden the scope of your search and start looking in second-hand stores or within the confines of your very own home. This means that, with a good wrapping job, you can finally get rid of that painting that your wife bought; a video that you never watch (now that you have a DVD player) or that houseplant that just never 'took off.' On the other hand, you could always go into your closet and pull out the 'Game Gift' that you got stuck with last year and recycle it into this year's game.

However you do it, you arrive at the appointed time with a wrapped gift, bringing us to:

Rule #2: Playing the Game. This is one of the simplest games in the world. One that even a six-year-old can play, which means that you are bound to spend an hour arguing over the rules. They are: Put all the gifts in the centre. Roll the dice. If you roll a 1 or a 6, pick a gift and unwrap it. Or don't unwrap it. Or simply choose to "steal" a gift from someone that has already chosen one.

Continue taking turns until everyone has a gift. Now the fun begins. Go to the kitchen and set the timer (you may also want to have the police on "stand-by"). Give yourself about two minutes and continue trying to roll ones or sixes. When you do, you are allowed to 'steal' from someone else and give them the gift that you have. 'Stealing' from your mate is not allowed. Unless it is.

When the timer goes off, the game is over. This means that, traditionally, most of the people in the group will beg for another minute so that they can get rid of the gift they have somehow ended up with.

Let me be honest with you, men. This is a very dangerous game to play when your spouse is involved. At some point in the activity, you will be asked to choose between grabbing the gift that you really want or going for something entirely useless (i.e. something that your wife really wants). At this point, the best thing to do is to be a man, stand up for your rights and fake an aneurism. Just last weekend we were in a situation where it was my turn to "steal" a gift. As I stood up, I could feel two desperate eyes drilling a hole into my back. I turned to see my wife staring at me, her expressionless face communicating reams of wordless messages and nuances that only a spouse of nine years would pick up on. "She's trying to tell me something," I thought. "I wonder what." Then, in a stroke of genius, I knew EXACTLY what she wanted. She wanted the candle that her sister had and it was my job to 'steal' it. Giving up my hopes of

62

owning my very own, battery-operated coin-sorter bank, I grabbed the candle and sat down.

Unfortunately, this did not stop my wife's desperate stares in my direction. In fact, if anything, her eyes got bigger. "Why would you take her candle from her? You knew she wanted it. Why didn't you grab the sleigh made out of barn board?"

Me: "THE SLEIGH?? YOU WANTED THE SLEIGH?? We've already got three sleighs in the living room! And they just sit there."

My wife (With a major eye-roll): "Never mind. You'd better replace her candle with something good or she'll never forgive you."

No problem. I hope she likes flatulent sound effects.

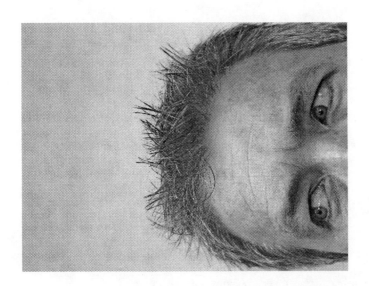

Muskoka Vacation

there are many different reasons for taking a vacation. You could lead a stressful life as a wildly popular humor columnist for a big community newspaper; your entire family-in-law may have planned a week's worth of relaxation and included you; OR your wife may have simply told you when SHE was going and expressed a hope that you might find time in your busy schedule to come along.

In my case, the reason was simple: we all had too much blood. My whole family was sitting around the coffee table one day noticing how bloated we were: "We need to go up north and get rid of some of this excess blood. Kids, start packing, we're going to Muskoka!"

Now, there are a few things to remember about Muskoka. The first is that its name comes from the Native word for "welts". Secondly, as part of the Canadian Shield, it is a place of immense beauty and peace. Thirdly, there are a lot of bugs.

As you drive north to Muskoka, you will notice some definite changes in scenery. Smokestacks and smog are replaced by pine trees and fresh air. Flashing neon signs and malls are replaced by the more natural landmarks of the North: lakes, hills and bait shops. Gladly, you will also notice that the headache of people driving bumper to bumper trying to get to work has been replaced by the headache of people driving bumper to bumper trying to get to their cottages, where they can relax.

Nothing compares to that feeling of having finally arrived at your destination. Oh the sights and sounds that greet you! Guaranteed, as soon as you step out of your minivan, you'll notice six, ten even twelve different types of flying parasites! And don't worry about missing any. Nature has everything organized like clockwork. Like little, unionized shift workers, you can count on being greeted by at least one (if not three or four) of nature's bloodsucking emissaries no matter when you're outside.

6am-8am Mosquitoes

8am-Noon Mosquitoes and Deerflies

Noon-5pm Deerflies, Blackflies and Horseflies (Beaches only)

5pm-8pm Mosquitoes and Deerflies

8pm-6am Mosquitoes

"No problem." You think to yourself. "I'll pack me some bug repellent."

With all due respect, you have the intelligence of a fish carcass. Muskoka bugs are not like our bugs. Our bugs may be irritating but at least they go away with a little shot of 'OFF' and the whisk of a hand. Muskoka bugs eat 'OFF' like you or I would eat candy floss. In fact, we brought THREE different kinds of repellent and nothing worked.

First, we tried Skin-So-Soft. This was a big mistake, mainly because Skin-So-Soft is a SKIN SOFTENER. For some reason, we were trying to use it as a REPELLENT. The bugs love this. "Look," they say," He's bathing in meat tenderizer. How thoughtful! Call Marge and the kids. It's time for a smorgasbord!"

Our next attempt was with the all-new, all-natural, sinus-clearing TEA TREE OIL. Trust me, the only thing this stuff keeps away is the other campers. Another dose of this and I would have been too flammable to roast marshmallows.

In desperation, we turned to an actual, chemical repellent containing DEET. Science only knows 2 things about DEET:

#1- As a chemical that might touch your skin, it is very bad.

#2- As a bug repellent, it is very good.

Unfortunately, Muskoka bugs were unaffected by DEET. In fact, I saw a deerfly chewing on a piece of raw DEET as one would a beef pepperette.

Luckily, over time we achieved equilibrium, a balance of sorts. We slowly noticed to our relief that we were getting bitten less and less to the degree that by the end of the week, we saw nary a probing proboscis.

66

Of course, it will be another two months before I can make a blood donation of any kind but by this time next year I should have enough extra saved up to necessitate another trip up north.

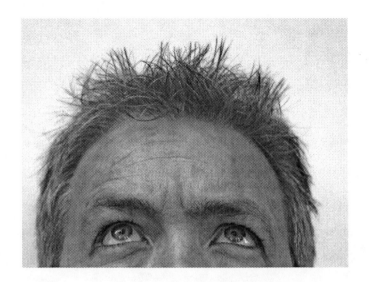

Putting The Man In Romance

the approach of SPRING marks the onset of the season of new beginnings. As green buds push through long-dormant branches and the sun presses warm water from the snow, the animal kingdom comes alive with the instinct to mate. Of course, some species don't wait until SPRING. One in particular seems to get its start somewhere around February fourteenth. As far as instinct goes, however, it's a wonder that these things reproduce AT ALL. In fact, just observing them offers a strong argument AGAINST natural selection and the notion of survival of the fittest. Maybe God just makes some things for His own entertainment.

The male of the species is the one to watch because his brain does not work. It is obvious that there is no connection between what he thinks of himself and any sort of reality. No matter what he looks like to the rest of the world, in his own mind he is an irresistible stud-muffin and the answer to every female's longing. This deception does not fade with age. In fact, the older, balder and fatter the single male gets, the more he seems to cling to whatever his faulty brain tells him. The real fun begins when you introduce a young, attractive female into a group of these older males. Immediately, their brains start lying to them, telling them they've got a shot. You will notice chests sticking out, huge guts being sucked in and all available hair being slicked back. Ironically, the female will be blissfully ignorant of all that is going on.

Strangely enough, when choosing a mate, the male is EXTREMELY picky. He may be an overweight slob and dress like he was attacked by a laundry hamper but the female he is waiting for must look like a Victoria's Secret model and be similarly attired. This is, after all, what his brain is telling him he deserves. Straying from this guideline in any way would be settling for "second best."

The actual mating ritual of this particular species is one that defies description (and common sense). You have to understand that even though he is now married, the man's brain is still not working properly. He can handle only a few thoughts per day, most of which are somehow related to the fact that it's time to get romantic with his wife. It doesn't matter what time of the day it is or if, in fact, his wife is in the same country. Once his brain delivers this message, off he goes to do what he can to make it happen. As a rule, 99.999% of the time, he fails miserably. This is why most guys subscribe to the myth of the "Holy Grail of Romance."

The Holy Grail of Romance is what keeps a man's spirits up after his one millionth failed attempt in a single day. It is the belief that there exists a single word or maybe a secret spot on her body that, when discovered and used, causes her to become his love slave. Fortunately for all involved, this is not the case. From my experience, if a man found out that, say, touching his wife's elbows caused her to become uncontrollably passionate, he would find a reason, not just every day but EVERY TEN MINUTES, to grab, touch and/or bump those elbows. Since we can say with a fair amount of accuracy that arm-joints don't do it for most women, husbands continue their quest by grabbing, touching and/ or bumping all parts of their wives in the hopes that, by playing the odds, they might finally enjoy a night of passion. What happens in reality is that their wives simply end up heavily calloused.

On the other hand, and as unbelievable as it may sound, romance to a lady involves talking, and lots of it. And I don't mean talking about anything that a normal male would consider "romantic." No, it seems that to get her in the mood her husband must ask her questions like, "How was your day?" AND ACTUALLY LISTEN TO THE ANSWER!!! Other popular topics of interest include: the "kids"; the financial state of the family; how she's "feeling" and how the house looks. This is beyond the scope of a man's understanding. He believes that in most cases, "talking" as a prelude to romance is an endurance test designed by his wife. She wants to see exactly how long he will continue engaging in conversation before he starts to cry.

Luckily, a woman's sympathetic nature will often overcome her, ensuring the propagation of the species and some rest for her calloused elbows.

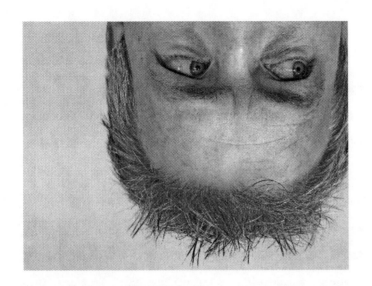

Remembering Granny

I n terms of straightforward coolness, no one comes close to a lady very near and dear to my heart: my Grandma. In fact, I would venture to say that everything I need to know, I learned from my Grandma. These important things include advice about right and wrong, manners and tips on saving money.

For instance, her philosophy in the kitchen was: "WHY SPEND MONEY ON TUPPERWARE WHEN YOU'VE GOT HUNDREDS OF PERFECTLY GOOD MARGARINE CONTAINERS JUST LYING AROUND?" So every time I went over for a meal, she would pull six or seven different faded plastic containers out of the fridge and put them in the microwave. None of us (including her) had a clue as to what was inside them, but that kind of made for a fun evening. It was a sort of blind buffet: "Wow, look at that! Ham, rice and something brown, all heated to microwaved perfection! DIG IN!" This prepared me for my career as a bachelor.

The more contact I had with Granny, the more I learned. It follows, then, that staying for holidays was like going to summer school, but to learn things I would actually find helpful in life. For instance, as a boy of eight years old I was a real novice when it came to handling curfews while away from home. Gram solved that problem by having NO CURFEW WHATSOEVER. In fact, the only way she knew it was time for me to go to bed was when I was already asleep on the floor. And watching Three's Company is okay at eight o'clock but if we waited just a few more hours, we could watch Jack Lord and his big hair wave on Hawaii Five Oh. And Buddy Ebsen in Barnaby Jones. And some really porcine guy as Cannon. And Oscar Madison as Quincy. Then I'd spend the next hour in bed alone, listening to all the sounds of the night, convinced someone wearing a dark leather glove was going to slowly open MY door, stick his hand into the room and shoot ME with a silencer. By morning I'd be exhausted but that was okay because Grandma always said: "IF YOU STAY UP LATE WATCHING TELEVISION, THE BEST THING TO DO IN THE MORNING IS SLEEP IN!"

Now I need to say right here that my grandmother was a church-going person. However, having grown up on the farm, she was also endowed with a vocabulary of words that one would find surprising for a little old lady. Her way of getting around any issues of appropriate language was to slightly change the pronunciation of the word in question, thereby tricking everyone. What does a cat do in the garden? It SHITES! I have to admit there were days when I would purposely bring up the subject of cats just to hear Grandma "swear."

Another pearl of wisdom that will long remain in my heart is this: "IT'S OKAY TO PASS WIND AS LONG AS YOU BLAME IT ON IMAGINARY ANIMALS." For as long as I can remember, my granny had this 'duck' that followed her everywhere. It was pretty much invisible but every once in a while, as she was walking down the hall, we would HEAR it and Gram would say, "Oh there's that duck again!" Try as we might, we never had so much as a partial sighting. In retrospect, while Granny's companion was a duck, it seemed my grandfather was stalked by a MOOSE. I have no idea how we could ever miss this creature who, by the sound of it, was the size of a house.

Of course, there were always conflicts that arose between the parents and the grandparents. This is because the grandparents wanted to do what was best for the child and the parents were all hung up on issues of discipline. But my grandmother always told me that when it came right down to the choice of whom to obey, your mother or your grandmother, ALWAYS OBEY YOUR MOTHER. THEN WHEN SHE LEAVES THE ROOM, GO TO YOUR GRANDMOTHER AND SHE'LL LET YOU HAVE WHAT YOU WANT. This seemed to work for everyone involved.

Yes, she had her unique qualities. She had a rocking chair that was the most powerful force known to man. None could sit in it with her for more than two minutes before falling into a dead slumber. Dining out meant KFC or, once a year, Chinese Food. And the best water in the world was bottled on a farm, two miles out of town. (Coinciden-tally when we were children growing up on that farm, the same water was going to be the death of us.) She knew the strangest songs and told the funniest stories about growing up in a world without televisions or cars. Knowing Grandma meant laughing a lot, crying just a little and if a sparkle in the eye could be inherited or at least transferred, we got ours from her. I will truly miss you for the rest of my life, Dorothy Isabel Healey. May you rest in peace.

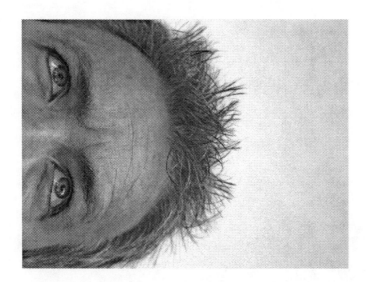

Dog Days
on the Catwalk

have no problem with "thinking outside of the box" when I decide to think at all. In fact, I like stretching myself and doing things that I've never done before. That is why, when my friend Kathy asked me to be a model at a charity fund-raiser, I agreed to it right away.

Kathy: "Are you sure?"

Me: "Yes."

Kathy: "You won't back out?"

Me: "No."

Kathy: "You mean it?"

Me: "Why are you still here?"

76

Now I know what you are thinking. You are thinking, "Mark, you are a suave and sophisticated Gad-About-Town with incredible style and panache. How is modeling thinking OUTSIDE of the box for you?" If that is what you are thinking, I have two things to say:

#1 Thank you, and…

#2 You must be new to this column.

While most of what you said is true, I must be honest in telling you that I'm not TOTALLY comfortable in the realm of "style." The reason for this is that, every so often, styles change. This is bad. I mean, if they were any good in the first place, why would they have to change? What's the big deal about change?

The fact that I have issues with "style" and "change" is the principle reason that my wife buys most of the clothes for the family. That is fine with me. The only demand I make is that I have LEVI jeans and white t-shirts, and an ample supply of both. To me, these are the only articles of clothing that I trust because they will stay "in" forever (or they may be "out" already and I don't know it).

Suffice to say, I don't do well with stylish clothes. In fact, I cannot be counted on to recognize what is stylish and what is not. In fact #2, my knowledge of current fashion is so minimal, someone could actually sign me up to model at a fashion show and dress me as a curried yam and I would walk out on stage, confident in the belief that I WAS STYLIN'! On the particular evening in question, however, this was not an issue. I was wearing actual clothes (that I would never, ever, ever in a million years pick out for myself) but looked and felt terrific. The evening was a success for several reasons: First, I looked HOT! and second, I DISCOVERED THE SECRET TO BEING A SUPERMODEL. Yes it's true. We all wonder how Supermodels do what they do.

How do they look so focused out there? How do they learn to do that special 'walk' on the catwalk, while strutting their stuff? That evening, as I prepared to display the clothing that I was wearing, I stumbled upon the answer and it assisted me in bringing the audience to its feet in applause and admiration (and, I think, laughter).

The secret is: DON'T GO TO THE BATHROOM.

Yes, it's true. Believe me. Nothing helps you focus more than knowing that if you're NOT done in fifteen seconds, you're going to drop a hem line, if you get my drift. Also, I discovered that trying to walk down a catwalk while crossing your legs AND clinching your butt cheeks together makes you look EXACTLY like the Supermodels we all know and admire. This also explains why Supermodels never have time for interviews after their shows. Its not that they're snobs, it's just that they are on their way to the little boys' room because THEY REALLY HAVE TO GO.

When I was finished, Kathy caught up to me.

Kathy: "Wow, Mark! You are awesome! I'm so proud, I think I'll bust!"

Me: "I know the feeling. Get out of my way!"

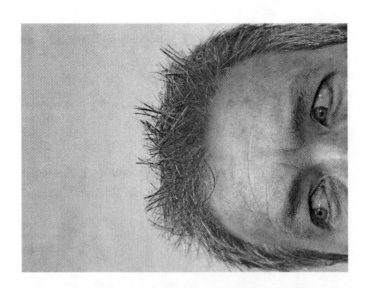

Clothes Make the Man...Crazy

" I bought you some more socks!"

This statement alone is a good indicator of the vast chasm between men and women. To be fair, the ENTIRE conversation went something like this:

My Wife: "I bought you some more socks!"

Me: "I needed socks?"

My Wife: (rolling her eyes) "Of course you did. I got you some light tan ones."

Me: "What would I use those for?"

My wife (rolling her eyes AND speaking slowly): "They are sort of in-between socks. You could wear them with your jeans, with your tan pants, with your deck shoes..."

80

Me: "I wear my white socks for that stuff."

My Wife: "I know. And do you remember someone making fun of you for that very reason?"

Me: "That doesn't count. It was your mother. Besides, my sock drawer is already full."

My Wife: "Not for long."

And thus begins the eternal cycle of fashion-replacement in our house. To her credit, my wife is incredibly patient and she faces the monumental task of getting me to look good. Actually, her challenge is even more difficult.

It is getting me to look good WHEN SHE'S NOT AROUND. It is every wife's fear that someday she will be dead and her husband will be heading to town in a suit jacket and plaid shorts, and dressing the children the same.

In my defence, I would like to say that I don't think my wife WANTS me to get into fashion mode. As long as I'm ignorant, she has carte blanche (translation: white socks) to buy whatever she thinks I need and she knows she won't get much of an argument.

So just when I think I'm catching on, "the rules change" or "the style fades". This serves to keep me in a state of constant confusion and forces me to rely on her unquestionable taste.

The frustrating thing for most guys is that we are not ones to let go of our clothes easily. Wives cannot understand this since, on any given day, they can be seen standing in front of their closet, sighing heavily and cursing the poor selection of choices they have. "Oh," they say, "I could never wear THAT!" as if every hanger held a prom dress from the late seventies. Guys, on the other hand, will still have (and wear) the concert t-shirt they bought in 1989. It is not that we hate our wives; it is simply a matter of trust. We trust our clothes. We trust our underclothes. In fact, I would go so far as to say that we love our boxers in a very special and intimate way. A way that will ensure we keep wearing them until they are not technically boxers anymore but several pieces of faded material held together by worn out thread molecules. We would actually experience more protection if we were to glue facial tissues to our fannies. Knowing this, my wife devised a plan whereby she would keep buying me boxers until my drawer was so full that I had no choice but to bid an emotional farewell to the oldest pairs. After that success, she moved on to my socks, t-shirts and pants, leaving me without a friend in the world (or my drawer). On a positive note, she has also stopped complaining about my skivvies and their state of disrepair. New clothes I can handle. I can do without the daily status reports on my underwear.

Now don't get me wrong. I am not saying that guys don't have any fashion sense. The odd ones do (ahem). I am merely pointing out that if our wives went on strike and absolutely refused to make sure we were properly dressed, we would somehow muddle through. We'd also become better friends with everyone in our drawers.

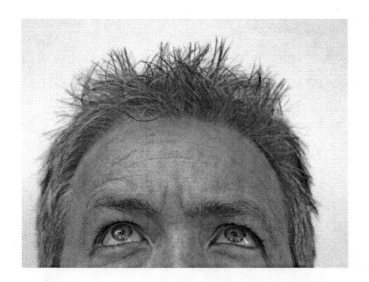

When Saturday Morning Meant Scooby Doo

the thing I miss the most about growing up is Saturday Morning Cartoons. Monday to Friday mornings we were the Walking Zombies from Watford with genuine corn syrup for blood. The first day of the Weekend, however, saw four young faces greeting dawn's early light with the blue screen of a '65 Zenith.

Those were the good old days: carefree yet strictly regimented. The typical schedule was as follows:

6:30 AM Wake up. Quietly sneaking downstairs will have its advantages: Mom and Dad will continue sleeping AND you will get full control over the TV guide.

84

6:34 AM Make noise roughly equal to an elephant stampede as all four children realize that each other is awake and race downstairs to be the first to the TV.

6:35 AM Turn the TV on.

6:36 AM Fix yourself a breakfast including one bowl of Cheerios with four spoonfuls of sugar and eighteen pieces of toast slathered in butter.

6:55 AM Your television has now warmed up to the point that the screen is hardly even moving up and down. Time to sit down and dig in.

7:00-8:00 AM SuperFriends/Bugs Bunny

8:04 AM No sign of Mom or Dad yet. Everyone is busy watching Scooby doo. You make a mental note to find out where "Daphne" goes to school.

8:30-12:00 PM Land Of The Lost/Fat Albert/Hong Kong Phooey/Rocket Robin Hood/Josie and the Pussycats/G-Force/Barba Papa

11:55 AM In five hours of programming, you have watched ten shows, fourteen School House Rocks segments (including Conjunction Junction), eighty-five commercials for new cereal and 146 spots for toothpaste. The latter are quite effective. In fact, before your parents have gotten out of bed, thanks to public broadcasting and some really gross pictures of tooth decay, you have brushed your teeth a total of nine times.

By the time your parents stumble out of their bedroom, their children are all in a sugar-and-media-induced stupor (we've never really climbed OUT of that stupor). All attempts at communication are futile.

Dad: "Where's the toothpaste ?"

Kids: "Conjunction Junction, what's your function...?"

Dad: "Hello. Could you all stop singing for a minute ? I need to know what happened to all the toothpaste. No, I do not know where "Daphne" lives."

Kids: "...binding up words and phrases..."

Dad: "Fine. I'm going to the store. I'll be right back."

Mom: "While you're there, you might as well pick up more bread. And milk. And butter. And sugar. And cereal."

You: "Cereal? CEREAL!! Dad, can you please,please,please buy us some SugarCornPops or FrostedLuckyCharms or AppleJacks or CountChocula or CocoaPebbles. They've got Eight Essential Nutrients."

Unfortunately (or fortunately), Dad never caved in and you were destined to spend the rest of your childhood dreaming about eating cereal loaded with enriched marshmallows. And sharing it with Daphne.

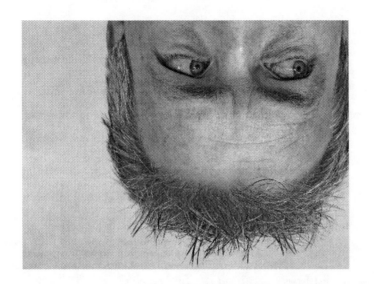

Karate Krisis

every year my wife and I have the same discussion. It's all about getting our children "involved". My wife sees various programs around the city and knows that each one holds an opportunity for our kids to learn social skills, to increase their physical activity and to have fun.

As for myself, I live in the dark world of reality, where I remember how much of a hassle it has always been to get our kids MOTIVATED to go to the programs they so desperately wanted to join months before. I remember the Dad (me) being told that it was Time To Go To Soccer and that I Had Better Get Ready. I also remember DRAGGING my screaming children into the van, then out of the van and onto the soccer field, sometimes while still in their pajamas.

88

"YOU ARE GOING TO PLAY SOCCER!" I would be yelling.
"YOU LOVE SOCCER! NOW. GET. OUT. THERE." Then I would
pry their fingers off of the van door and hurl them onto the grass. I was
not the only one, either. If you drive into a soccer parking lot, you will
be amazed at how many minivans have long, deep claw marks down the
side. Those memories are vivid and fresh in my mind and they prevent
me from getting excited about signing up for more. My wife's memory
is not as long. I know this because she opted to have two more children,
even after she discovered first-hand how the first one arrived.

Still, some activities are better than others. At least with soccer, your
kids learn a skill that could prove useful for starting a riot in Europe. With
others, you may not be so lucky!

My Wife: "I think I'll sign our son up for Karate."

Me: "Who? The baby?"

My Wife: "No. Our oldest son."

Me: "You're kidding, right?"

My Wife: "What do you mean?"

Me: "Our oldest son is the one who spends a half an hour a day on 'time-
outs'. You want to show him how to use his body as a weapon? Why not
teach a hurricane how to handle dynamite?"

My Wife: "It's only a hundred bucks. I've already sent the form in."

Me: "A HUNDRED BUCKS?? You mean we have to PAY to teach him how to be an efficient killer?"

My Wife: "It'll be a good distraction for him. It will take up those two hours a week when he's not teasing his sister."

Hoping that Karate would rid him of his excess energy, I agreed to accompany him to his first class. In other words, I was told by his mother that I would be accompanying him to his first class. The instructor was kind enough to provide us with a translation for some basic Karate terms:

Jet-Ski: Line up!

Soiled Knee: Bow down!

Itchy: One

Knee: Two (giving someone the 'old one-two' is referred to as the 'old itchy knee')

Sun: Three

Chi: Four

Go: Five

Rook You: Six (ironically, the registration form is known as Form Six)

Titchy: Seven

Hatchy: Eight

90

Coo: Nine

Jujube: Ten

The Instructor: "Welcome to Karate! Those of you who are new will notice that in Karate, there are different colors of belts that you can wear. Each belt symbolizes a degree of difficulty. If you stay in this class, you will no longer lash out in a blind rage when frustrated. I will show you, through study and discipline, how to lash out in a focused and measured rage. Let us begin."

When we arrived home, my wife was interested in what the class was like.

My Wife: "So how did it go?"

Me: "Well, one thing's for sure. I don't think we'll have any problems with motivation."

My Wife: "Great!!"

Me: "And I think it would be best if his sister moved out of the house for a while. Or maybe took up Karate herself."

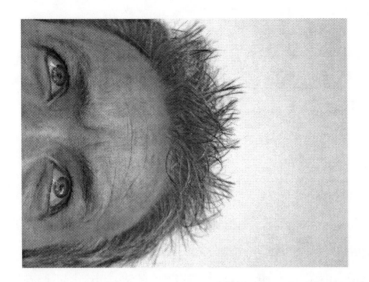

Kids and Colds

You know, if I had my way, I'd pull my kids right out of school. That way, they'd be ignorant, but very healthy. As it is, our house is a constant parade of the Disease Of The Week! The kids come home with anything and everything, including, I believe, scurvy. And one by one, I watch it spread, first from child to child, then from child to parent, then from parent to parent. Then when the virus has gone through the entire family, it is time to send the kids BACK to school to recharge!

That is exactly why I decided not to be a teacher. Well, that and the fact that I'm allergic to #2 pencils.

Anyway, the point of this rant is that I send my children to school for the express purpose of getting an education so they can buy me a house they're older. I do not send them to school to grow a perma-ring of dried booger around their nostrils. How is that going to help me?

92

If your kids are not yet in school, let me tell you something: From the day that they enter kindergarten, their noses will not stop running until the day they graduate from university. Oh, it will slow down (from a handful to a finger full), but don't think it will ever stop completely!

Why does this happen? Why is it so easy for our kids to pick up so many viruses? To answer these questions, it is important not to "lay blame" or look for a "scapegoat". For instance, as a parent, you may feel compelled to point out the fact that there are certain children who are sent to school with no winter apparel at all. This is not proof of poor parenting; this is simply someone's way of helping their kids to "think positive".

Parent: "Son, I know that good health is all a matter of good thoughts. To prove it, I'm going to hide your parka. Good luck."

Son: "Thanks, dad. HAH-CHOOO!!"

Parent: "Wipe that up. And for heaven's sake, think better thoughts."

You may also want to blame children who pick their noses for the fact that your kids get sick. Let's face it. Kids are dumb. They don't care how clean something is before they put it in their mouths or share it with their friends. That's why God invented parents. And Lysol. And the Swiffer. And don't get all down on the kid who is running around outside with his finger up his nose. He's only doing what he has to do to keep his hands warm because his dad hid his mittens.

In the end, I believe that it is the teacher's responsibility to stop the spread of disease in its tracks. They should be equipped to sterilize each student as they enter the class, much like restaurants sterilize dishes. And I think they should show a safety film like: "Peter Pointer Gets Stuck in the Haunted Nose Cave." For it is only when we take these things seriously that we will begin to turn the tide and win this so-called War of the Noses.

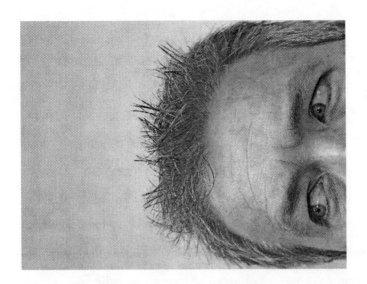

Mark's Close Friend Hits The Road

dear Friend,

You have to appreciate how difficult it is to write this letter. Especially since I know that you can't read and I couldn't be bothered just talking to you face to face. I want you to know that it has been exactly eight years since we met and those have been some of the happiest years of my life. But life moves on. We age. You in particular have aged a lot. And not very well.

Don't be mistaken. It's not that I don't love you. I will always treasure your memory. It's just that it's tough to get you going in the morning and by evening you are definitely ready for the day to be done.

Do you remember when you first saw me? You were young, energetic and ready for action! I know that I've changed since then as well but,

96

quite frankly, I can do that without fear of being replaced by something newer and sexier. Sadly, you cannot.

Oh, I know what you're thinking. You're thinking that I won't UNDERSTAND the new models out there. That maybe they're a little too complex for my simple ways. Well you may be right. But let me be honest with you and say that there was a lot I didn't understand about you as well, and we got along just fine! How did you make those seatbelts move when I opened the door, even for a second? I couldn't tell you! Are you front wheel drive or back wheel drive? How many cylinders are you running on? What do all those numbers on your tires mean? Beats me! I open the "hood" and see "1.9 SEFI" engraved on the top of the engine block thingy. What does this mean? I don't know but I would hazard a guess that it stands for: Something, Everything. Fine Investment! That's what you were to me: a fine investment. Yes, you were only a little red Escort but you were a hard worker who never let me down. You racked up 280,000 kilometres without a problem or complaint and now it's time for me to end our relationship.

Will it be hard, writing that classified ad begging someone to take you off my hands? You bet! Will it be tough getting out there again, learning new names like Taureg, Focus and Elantra? Oh yeah! But I will survive! You have taught me what to appreciate in a fine automobile and in the end I realize that it is I who does not deserve you. It is time for us both to move on. Me to a hot new set of wheels and you to the auto wreckers where you can get the rest you deserve until they crush you into a tiny box.

We will meet again, you and I. Maybe you'll be a toaster oven or an integral part of a landfill. I'll know you. I could pick you out of a crowd a mile away. That's why my next car will be the same colour as you: red. Or maybe silver. Or another colour. In honour of you.

My car.

Sincerely Yours For Now,

Mark

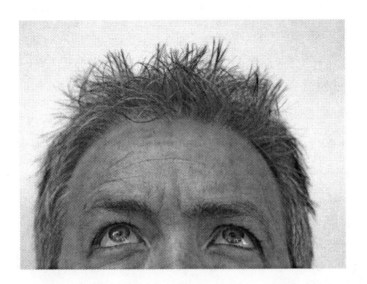

Hip to Country Music

S o, let's get something straight right off the bat: I do not consider myself a listener of what you would call Country Music. I don't have a problem with it, mind you, it's just not my cup of tea (or in Country Music lingo: my mug of beer). But I have to say that a few weeks ago I was scanning the stations and came across this song that I ABSOLUTELY HAD TO KEEP LISTENING TO. I had no idea what station it was on or who was singing it but, man oh man, it was quite a good tune (Country Music translation: a real humdinger). Now the station really knew what it was doing because they never announced the name of the band. If they had, I would have simply bought the CD and been on my way. As it turned out, I was forced to listen at every chance I got–in my car, in my home, in my office with my door closed while I was supposed to be working, etc. The more I tuned in, the more I was forced to listen to all kinds of different songs- some good, some… not so much, and every thirty-six hours or so, they would tease me with THE SONG that I was looking for. It only took a few minutes of ear-straining to realize that I had found a "Country Music Station". What I hadn't found, however, was the name of the band OR their song.

Finally, out of sheer desperation I did something that I absolutely hated to do: I phoned my sister-in-law and asked for help.

Me: "You listen to (ahem) "Country" don't you?"

Holly: "Yes. Why are you whispering?"

Me: "Well, I accidentally listened to it the other day. I didn't mean to but I did and now I'm addicted. I can't get enough of this one song. Can you help me?"

Holly: "You need therapy."

Anyways, I finally found out what I needed to know. The song is "Save a Horse" by the band Big and Rich. I bought the CD. It's good. Now I have a different problem. Now that I have the CD, should I continue listening to the Country Music station? Should I program it into my car stereo? Do I know how to do that? Here are the Pros and Cons of converting:

I should listen to Country Music because:

I like wearing jeans. I can yell "YEE-HAW". I grew up on a farm. It's easy to listen to. I think HEE-HAW was funny. I actually own a pair of cowboy boots. Shania Twain. Cowboys are fairly cool.

I shouldn't listen to Country Music because: I don't drink beer. I'm not allowed to wear my cowboy boots. I can't spit. I don't think HEE-HAW was THAT funny. Willie Nelson. Line Dancing. I don't watch NASCAR. Rednecks are fairly dorky. This whole dilemma (Country Music translation: perdinkament) brings me right back to my roots. Even though I grew up in rural Ontario, my parents made sure that I got all the culture I could handle. It came out of the clock radio on top of the fridge: George Jones, Charley Pride, Ray Price, Loretta Lynn and the incomparable (!) Anne Murray. So I called my Dad for some advice.

Me: "Dad, I'm thinking of starting to tune in to Country Music. Any thoughts?"

My Dad: "I'd go for it if I were you. I've been listenin' since Adam was a pup and look what its done fer me."

Me: "Well, that point right there is all I really need."

Hello, Rock and Roll

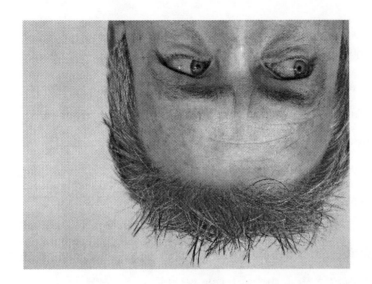

Love Marches to the Golden Arches

ivorce in this country has reached epidemic proportions. If something isn't done to fix the problem, there will soon be no one in the local McDonalds but bitter men and women trading their kids back and forth. This is why they invented Happy Meals.

Long ago, before midriff-baring t-shirts and MTV, you had to date your partner for a long time, like, say, eight to ten years. THEN you had to Meet The Parents and prove to them (via a slide rule) that you had the financial wherewithal to support your loved one for the rest of her life. The rules were so strict back then that you might not have even known what she LOOKED LIKE for sure. Yet somehow, these people managed to stay together for fifty, sixty, even a hundred years. Since that is not the way things are today, obviously we are missing something. I don't think that it is intimate knowledge of well, you know, how to be "intimate". I believe that is now an elective in high school. The main reason for divorce in this country is that somehow we keep marrying people who are faulty. Ask any woman why she divorced her husband and she'll tell you, "He was a (expletive) (expletive) idiot!" Her ex. will have similar opinions about her: "AAUUGH! She was such a (expletive)!!" So we need to either find a solution to divorce or risk totally running out of expletives to describe our relationships.

One small step would be in the marriage ceremony itself. Maybe what we need is Marriage Vows that are more realistic. I mean, what does "For Better or Worse, In Sickness and in Health" really tell you? Nothing! I propose the Life 101 Guide to Eye-Opening Marriage Vows. They would go something like this:

The Pastor: "Herb Flounder, do you hereby take this woman to be your wife? Do you know how cold her feet can get and where she's going to stick them? Will you love her even though she can't burp in bed without sitting up? Do you realize that she has a vivid imagination that only applies to terrible things that could happen if you let the kids out of your sight or if you don't investigate every sound in the dead of the night? Are you aware that she will become obsessed with smelling things ranging from your arm hair to your children's lunch bags and everything in between? Do you realize that when you finally have children, even though you are in her heart, your kids will always be on her mind? Are you okay with the fact that there will be two ways to locate her in your house: #1 By following the trail of lights that are still on or #2 By where all the stomping and door-slamming is coming from? And how do you plan to react when she spends $200 on new drapes (We need new drapes?) for the living room but gives you the evil eye over the newest version of "HALO"? Let's not forget that after four or five kids, she is going to look NOTHING like she does right now, despite the hints that you drop and you will never NEVER want to see her in a two piece bathing suit again. Are you still interested?"

Herb: "Well, I..."

The Pastor: "And you, Bertha Vanhooydonk, are you aware of your future husband's lack of fashion sense AND the fact that he will resist your many, many, many attempts to transplant one within him? How does it feel, knowing that he HATES being told what to do and even though he may have been going to do that very thing anyways, he will stop and do something else just to prove that you are not the boss of him? Are you okay with the fact that he will throw the dish cloth directly into the greasy frying pan that you are soaking in the sink? And how will you react when he turns his nose up at the meal you have been slaving over all day and THEN suggests "something good" like Kraft Dinner? Do you know that he will be TOTALLY ENGROSSED in a movie until they get to the romantic part, and then you won't be able to shut him up? And do you realize that he will leave phone numbers on tiny scraps of paper as well as all sorts of lists and receipts all over the house AND EXPECT YOU TO KEEP TRACK OF THEM? And don't forget that in about

106

ten years, his gut will be hanging over his belt and his hair will be leaving his scalp and migrating to his ear sockets! Should we keep going?"

Bertha: "Come to think of it..."

On second thought, to make things even easier all first dates should begin at McDonalds.

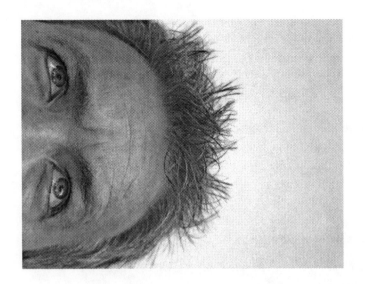

Family Milestones

the other day my wife mentioned to me that we were at another milestone in our career as a family: "It's time to toilet train the baby." I had the typical guy reaction: "Huh." You see, as a guy, and especially as a guy who is a husband, you cannot be too careful when you respond to ANYTHING your wife tells you. She may tell you that she didn't have time to make a casserole for dinner so you'll have to have Kraft Dinner and hotdogs. "Great!" you'll say, only to watch your wife collapse on the couch and start weeping. "Don't you LIKE my casseroles?" she'll ask. "I try so hard to stay on top of everything in this house and nobody appreciates anything I do!" To which you reply, "Huh" and slowly back out of the room.

That is why I responded the way I did to my wife's announcement. After eleven years of marriage, I am proud to say that 'responding' is one

108

of my greatest talents and other husbands could learn from my example. I'll give you the replay:

My Wife: "It's time to toilet train the baby."

Me (biting my lip thoughtfully): "Huh."

Then I looked at her in a Meaningful Way to let her know that I am 'with her' in whatever way I can be without having to actually peel poopy pants off of a squirming two-year old. "Don't forget I'll be at work that week. I may even have to stay overnight." Those are the ideas that my Meaningful Look conveyed.

Overall, however, I'd have to say that I am quite happy to be moving out of the diaper stage. Not only was changing diapers an inconvenience ("I'm going to the office again!"), not changing them reminds me that we are one step closer to my goal of Having The House To Ourselves. Most guys my age have been dreaming about this stage in life since, well, our first baby came home. Once we get all the kids out of the house, there will be one less objection that our wives can offer up as we try to Make Our Move: "No Honey, the kids are just downstairs/upstairs/in the next room/waking up/going to sleep."

The female point of view on this subject is predictable. Even the idea that her children, the ones she carried around INSIDE OF HER, are growing up will start her crying and bemoaning the fact that time flies too quickly and they'll soon be gone "forever". Then she'll decide that the kids don't have to leave home when they go to college. They can live at home and their father can drive them back and forth every day, even if they live in Canada and the college in question is not, technically, on the same continent.

Husbands are well aware that their carefully laid plans may well be for naught. By the time the last one is out of the house, the first one could be calling up, asking if Grandma and Grandpa will baby-sit for the weekend so that Mommy and Daddy can have the house to themselves.

To which Grandpa will reply:

"Huh."

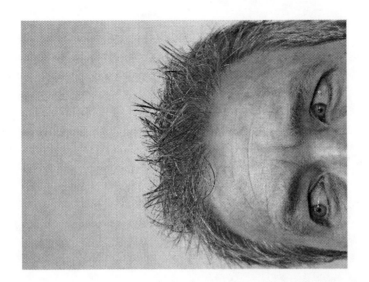

Wheels Inn

every once in a while, no matter how busy you are, you need to pack up the family for a vacation. If your wife catches on to the fact that you don't intend to go WITH the family, you may be in trouble. The best backup plan is to make sure that the family is going somewhere fun, so that you will enjoy yourself if you have to join them. Remember, you must try to get the best value for your dollar wherever you go, so see if you can get someone else to pay for the trip. (I highly suggest the children's grandparents.)

Last weekend was such a weekend for the Thrice family. We decided, after much debate and research, that we would go to a place called 'The Wheels Inn' in Chatham, Ontario. (To be honest, there was no debate. In fact the entire conversation lasted about four minutes.)

112

My Wife: "Honey, my parents want to take us to The Wheels Inn for a holiday."

Me: "Well, we have lots to do around here. I was hoping to work some more on the back yard..."

My Wife: "They're paying."

Me: "I'll go pack."

The thing that you, the unlearned public, probably don't know about The Wheels Inn is that it is a child's paradise. Not only is there a POOL, there is also a WATERSLIDE. And a ROLLERCOASTER. And a FERRIS WHEEL and a BOWLING ALLEY and Canada's biggest JUNGLE GYM and a MINI-GOLF RANGE and about 500 ARCADE GAMES! Yes, one could really have a good time in a place like this if one didn't feel so guilty about keeping the kids locked in the hotel room.

But it was definitely a holiday full of adventure and discovery. In fact, the first discovery we made as we arrived was that there was a girls' hockey tournament in town AND THEY WERE ALL STAYING AT OUR HOTEL.

Our next amazing discovery was that this tournament included some American teams. Imagine a hotel parking lot filled with minivans, decorated to make their northern neighbours sit up and pay attention. Slogans like "Red Whings Rule!" caught many a Canadian eye and reminded us with whom who we were dealing. Luckily, many of us were bilingual and were able to help our southern allies when they referred to things such as "hah-key" and "Tim Hawtons."

I do not know a lot about girls OR hockey. Thankfully, someone does and let me assure you that those "someones" had a strict regimen of training in force, even in the hotel. I was not privy to the ENTIRE program, but I did manage to catch a part of the action and I can't tell you how impressed I was. The most important part of the training exercise was Pushing All The Buttons In The Elevator. This was the hardest event and, as such, required the most practice. The athletes had to enter the elevator, select all the floors AND exit the elevator without being seen. While this was more of an effort in strategy, other exercises focused on agility and strength. Of course, I'm referring to the "Ride The Baggage Carts Through Unsuspecting Families" game as well as the Chase Each Other Through All Ten Floors Of The Hotel Game.

Now I know what you are thinking. You are thinking "Sheesh Mark! You put the 'Fuddy' in 'Fuddy-Duddy'!" To which I would reply: "There is no such word as 'Fuddy'." Also, there is a difference between what these girls were doing and what I would have done at that age. True, we may have been just as wild and just as silly. We may have done EXACTLY the same childish tricks, but believe me, if WE did them, they would have been funnier. Plus, if it was a team of boys, you could sure count on less giggling and a lot more belching and farting. Especially in the halls. That is what has made this country's national sports program what it is today.

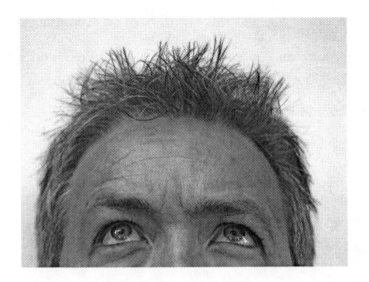

Selective Hearing

they say that once you start having kids, your life will never be the same. This is true. For one thing, you have given yourself more people to answer to and more people to call on you both day and night. However, I have recently developed a condition that gives me a new freedom: freedom to continue my activities without interruption; freedom to claim ignorance about most of the things that go on in our house and, most importantly, freedom to sleep through the night.

The condition? I have contracted a serious case of Selective Hearing. And apparently, I am in very good company since both my father and father-in-law have exactly the same problem. Even though this disease has severely limited my usefulness as the "go-to" guy in our house, I am doing fine. Or WAS until my wife developed her own "treatment" for me. You see, during the day, my wife doesn't really care if I heard her the first, second or thirty-third time. She will keep at me until I do what she wants me to do. However, at three A.M., it is not expedient to grab a guy by the ears and holler into his face. So when one of our little cherubs is awake, it is faster for her to get out of bed than it is for her to try to wake me up.

Unfortunately, she has come up with several different ways to make sure that, if I am sleeping, at least it won't be soundly.

CROWDING THE GUY

In our bedroom we have a large bed. It is fairly comfortable and has more than enough space for two people. The reason that it is so roomy is simple: no one sleeps on her side. It's true. When I slip between the sheets I find her already on my side of the bed waiting for me so that she has someplace to stick her frigid toes. I am not allowed to cross the line onto her side of the bed. Any attempt meets with stiff resistance.

Me: "Why am I not allowed to stretch onto your side of the bed? YOU are always on MY side."

My Wife: "That's different. You like it."

FREEZING THE GUY

Let me tell you something. I can get out of bed without waking my partner. I can slide out the side of the blankets and leave them in place so that she doesn't catch a chill while she slumbers. I can even feel my way down the hall without the aid of a light and not get hurt. Unfortunately, none of these facts hold true for the love of my life. I am well aware every time the baby wakes up because his mother loudly curses him as the fruit of MY loins. I know EXACTLY how many times she has to get OUT of bed because it corresponds to the number of times that I have to pull the blankets up from my ankles again. And I know how many times she RETURNS to bed because it would be the same number of times that she buries her cold appendages somewhere in my warm person.

I am also privy to her location in the house because she leaves a trail of light behind her wherever she goes, starting with the lamp on the bedside table. In fact, if it weren't for light switches in our house, I would have no idea if my sweetheart was even home.

TORTURING THE GUY

I wouldn't call it "snoring" exactly. Somehow, though, my wife has managed to copy the sound of someone sawing wet plywood. It starts quietly in the bottom of her throat and, after only an hour, works its way out for all to enjoy. This not only wakes a fellow up, it also helps clear his sinuses.

My Wife: "How was your sleep last night?"

Me: "Terrible. After the kids finally went back to sleep you started snoring. I tried to wake you but it was like you couldn't even hear me."

My Wife: "You don't say!"

119

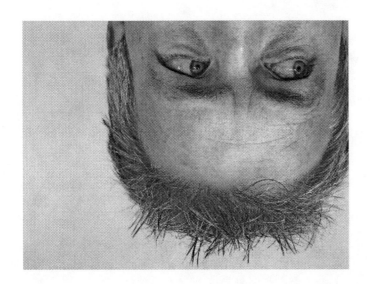

To Tell the Truth,
I Swear

O
ne of the great things about watching our kids grow up is
knowing that they can finally communicate with us on a
civilized level. Well, they're getting

closer anyways. At least we know that with the older two, we are
gradually getting away from conversations like this:

Your Child: "Barney!"

You: "Yes. Barney the Dinosaur."

Your Child: "Barney!"

You: "Yes! Barney is a dinosaur. Isn't he silly?"

Your Child: "Barney!"

120

You: "Silly Barney! Can you say Silly Barney?"

Your Child: "Barney!"

You: "Good Boy!"

In fact, my wife and I were just discussing in the van how far our children have come when my oldest son interrupted me:

My Son: "Dad, I know the "F" word."

Me: "You know what word?"

My Son: "The "F" word. You know...THE "F" WORD."
    --(Sound of tires screeching to a halt)--

Me: "Where did you learn that?"

My Son: "In school."

Me: "Well, finally our education system has helped our kids be first in something. Stupid school."

My Wife: "Honey, don't blame the school. He probably learned it from his friends at recess."

Me: "Stupid friends."

My Wife: "Oh, honey...it's not their fault either. They're just repeating what they hear at home from their parents....Stupid Parents!" The day was far from over. My son's curiosity (which he got from his mother's side) finally got the best of him.

My Son: "Dad, what does it mean?"

Me: "What?"

My Son: "You know. The "F" word. What does it mean?"

Me: "Nothing."

My Son: "DAD! It's a word. It has to mean something. Just tell me."

Me: "It doesn't mean anything. THAT'S why they made it into a swear word."

My Son: "I also know the "A" word."

Me: "Great."

My Son: "And the "S" word."

Me: "Mmm–hmm"

My Son: "Dad..."

Me: "What?"

My Son: "Are there any other words?"

Me: "I don't think so."

122

My Son: "Is there a "B" word?"

Me: "No."

My Son: "Is there a "C" word?"

Me: "Definitely not."

My Son: "So I know all of them?"

Me: "Believe me son, you are way ahead of where I was at your age." When things cool down over here, I'll call the other parents and give them a piece of my mind. I guess I've got plenty of time to choose my words carefully.

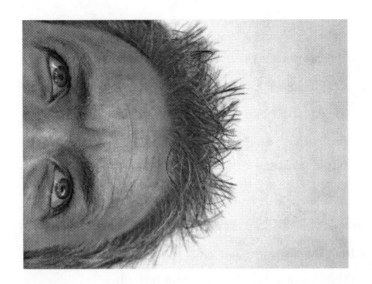

Trouble Over Bridged Waters

the worst thing about being a parent, especially a dad, is the fact that for all intents and purposes, the buck stops here. ("Here" being exactly where you are sitting at the time.) This is especially true when it comes to the children's education. Oh, you can complain that teachers can't teach and that it's their responsibility to do EXACTLY WHAT YOU PAY THEM THEIR OUTRAGEOUS SALARY TO DO. But when it comes right down to it, they (the children) are yours (as far as you know) and it's your job to get them to fall in love with learning. Besides, if your wife ever heard you griping, she'd think that you were shirking your duties and you would get ZERO lovin' for a week. (Since, as we all know, duty-shirking and lovin' are inversely proportionate.)

Having said that, it was with great angst that I approached last Sunday. Mainly because it was the LAST Sunday that my son had to work on his School Project before it was due. Let me just say right now that there are several Flaws inherent in the whole idea of a School Project. First of all, there is a communication Flaw. The Teacher gives a Project to the Student who takes it home to the Parent for help. The problem lies in the fact that the Teacher does not CALL the Parent to say, "Two weeks ago I gave your son this project where he has to build a bridge and it is due in THREE DAYS. Good luck!" No. Instead, you find out about it when you help the boy clean out his backpack; on your way to the garbage can to throw out two days' worth of bread crusts and orange peels, you uncrumple a juice-stained sheet of paper and read the bad news yourself.

The next Flaw concerns the fact that knowledge is power. Since your son is the only one who REALLY knows what is going on, he installs himself as foreman on a job you can't turn down without serious romantic implications. He uses this power with impunity and gives out information on a "need to know" basis.

Me: "Okay, so we have to build one of the bridges on this sheet for your project."

My Son: "Right."

Me: "These are all fairly complicated bridges. Let's go get your Tinkertoy."

My Son: "The teacher said we can't use anything like that. We have to use all original materials."

Me: "Perfect. Just what I wanted to do with my Sunday evening."

My Wife: "What was that?"

Me: "I said, 'This should be a great project this evening!'"

My Son: "Okay. I think I want to build a Draw Bridge."

Me: "There is no 'Draw Bridge' on this sheet."

My Son: "Yeah, well, we don't HAVE TO build one off the sheet."

Me: "...I see. Well, this will be easy. Go get some scissors and some paper."

My Son: "Yeah, only the bridges have to support weights that the teacher puts on them."

Me: "...Any other detail you'd care to let me in on?"

My Son: "Did I tell you it's due tomorrow?"

Me: "I can't believe I pay taxes for this. Alright. Go get a cardboard box and some scissors and prepare to be amazed!"

My Wife: "Remember, he has to do this himself."

Me: "You know, that sounds so promising...yet, here I am."

   After a few hours of construction, the project was completed.

My Son: "I think I really learned something from this project."

126

Me: "What was that? How important it is to communicate? How it's a good idea to get started early?"

My Son: "No. How cool it is to be the boss! I can hardly wait for my next project!"

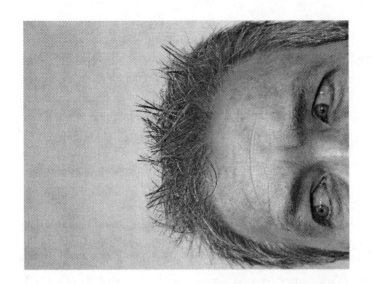

The Stages of Chicken Pox

there is a good way to change your attitude about your job. If you find that every morning is a struggle to pull yourself out of bed (assuming that you, unlike 97 percent of the people in THIS city, do NOT do shift work in the Chemical Valley and have a normal, decent job working for peanuts);if you face a day of work with the same fervor and zeal that you face, for instance, a "full" physical, there is hope. I can tell you what it is in two words:

White Slavery.

HO! Just Kidding!

I really meant to say: Chicken Pox!

That's right. Chicken Pox. The disease that will have such a porfound impact on you that you will have no problem BOUNDING out of bed and streaking off to work. (Of course, you'll come back down when you realize that, in your haste to leave, you literally were "streaking" off to work, and besides, it's Sunday and the office is closed.) Chicken pox, or Varicella (from the Latin: Night of the Living Dead) is caused by coming into contact with someone else who has it. Once the virus gets inside you, it enters the incubation period, much like the carnivorous parasite in ALIEN. That lasts for 11-21 days. Then you break out into a rash, characterized by pustules. That goes on for 35-76 days. The pustules scab over (16 days) and fall off (3 days) and the rash fades away (two years and seven months). During this whole time your body is itchy, as if little ants live directly beneath your skin. (Note: never use this analogy in the presence of the sick child.)

The worst part of it, though, is what it does to your family. Headaches, crying, screaming, grumpiness, loss of appetite. And that's just for the parents. It may be worse for the kids who actually HAVE the disease. Consider this fair warning.

STAGE ONE

The child may seem unnaturally irritable. He may be lethargic and keep to himself but more likely he'll start quoting dialogue from "The Shining" and take an interest in kick-boxing. This is a good time to leave him at your parents' place and go for a week-long excursion to Bora Bora. He is now contagious.

STAGE TWO

Red blotches now cover your child's body. You're the parent so you try to pretend that you don't notice anything out of the ordinary. Your child believes you until your wife sees him and screams. Your child is still contagious.

STAGE THREE

It has now been two months since your wife has had any contact with the outside world. She hates you for holding a job. You know this because she has started storing all the dirty diapers in the underwear drawer. Although his rash appears to be clearing up, you find that you're actually sleeping less than before. You convince yourself that there must be SOME benefits to waking up every fifteen minutes. The lack of sleep has had little effect on you except for the fact that you now weep uncontrollably at all traffic signals. Your child is still contagious.

STAGE FOUR

All scabs have fallen off. The boy is sleeping peacefully. Grandpa says something innocent like, "Well, that wasn't so bad," and your wife screams.

Evaluating Life
Post-Secondary School

t is time, once again, for the famous Watford High School Reunion. Fifteen years of post secondary life offer a chance to look back and "take stock". By "taking stock" I mean comparing my ambitions then to what I've gotten myself into now.

1) When I get older, I will be married and we will be romancing like untamed primates.

Now, before any of you "experienced" husbands (or wives) laugh your experienced heads off, let me remind you that for me, high school was still "pre-puberty". While all my friends were making secret visits to the Hormone Store then heading straight to the darkened corners of the dance floor for "Grope Fest '82", I was timidly watching MAGNUM P.I. and perfecting my technique for making fart noises with my armpit.

132

As a young male with virtually NO body hair, I would go to school the next day and have to endure all of the "war stories" about the previous night, as told by about 85 percent of my friends. My only consolation was swearing that when I finally found a girl, the romping would start at the altar and carry me right through to retirement.

In reality, we all know that there can be a plethora of obstacles to one's love life. Obstacles one would never think of in a co-ed Physical Education class. Things like fatigue, sick kids, full schedules, sick kids that are fatigued, money problems and being fatigued because your kids are sick, stressed and wearing fatigues.

When life presents you with one of these insurmountable obstacles, be a Sensitive and Mature Guy. Kiss your wife gently and spend the remainder of the evening watching reruns of MAGNUM P.I.

2) When I finally get out on my own, I'm going to make the world Stand Up and Take Notice.

This, of course, was a promise made by virtually every student in high school, even the ones who were sober. And, in fact, it turned out to be true. The world did take notice. As soon as I got "out there" they took notice that my rent was due, as were my student loan and car payments. The fact that I was really a lot of fun at parties and had quite a few ideas to share didn't matter so much because nobody was, technically, listening.

3) Who cares what kind of job I get? Anything is better than school!

If I could go back in time I would return to Watford High School and kick my stupid self in the butt. What job gives you an hour a day to exercise and whip basketballs at each other? How about two weeks at Christmas and the entire summer OFF to go camping and impress girls at the beach? And, as far as my extensive post-graduate research concluded, there are very few corporations, if any, that offer a "spare".

On the other hand, maybe I've got it all wrong. Maybe my former classmates will show me how to trade my current profession of writing highly unreliable columns for something much more lucrative.

Or we could (and I believe that this is what will actually happen) spend the whole night around the campfire making fart noises with our armpits.

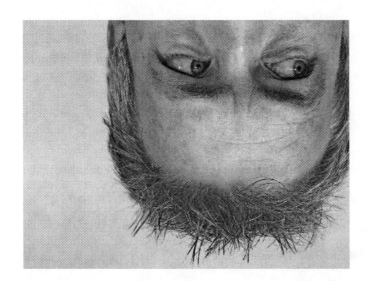

Cool 101

every guy, no matter how old, wants to be cool. Then he has kids. Before long, he is changing poopy diapers, wiping snotty noses with his bare hand and listening to Sesame Street Songs all the way up to the cottage. This will suck the cool out of him like a Hoover on a dust bunny. And before he gets a chance to start building up his Coolness Reserves his kids start to get older and realize what a GOMER they have for a father. They will hold this opinion until they have children of their own. The problem is that there is always someone older around to impress them.

My Kids: "Great Grandpa lived in Siberia and rode horses everywhere. Did you?"

Me: "Well, no, not exactly."

136

My Kids: "Papa was born during the war and built his own race car to drive around in. Did you?"

Me: "Alright. Time for bed."

Luckily for me, my kids have discovered something that sets me apart and makes me cooler than my father and grandfather combined. Yes, they now realize that in my youth I lived life on the edge. I took it to the limit. I laughed in the face of certain death.

My Son: "So, when you were little, you NEVER wore a seat belt AT ALL?"

Me: "That's right. And on special occasions, my dad would let me ride up in the back window."

My Son: "Did you die?"

Me: "A couple of times."

My Son: "WOW!!"

Me: "Plus, when we had to take the truck to town, we'd get to ride in the BACK!"

My Daughter: "Did you wear your helmet?"

Me: "Didn't have a helmet, even for our bikes. Sometimes we'd land on our heads and have to get up and keep riding. That's how tough we were."

My Son: "Were you even tough as a baby?"

Me: "HA! Let me tell you something. When I was a baby, the bars on my crib were spaced just wide enough to get your head through...but not wide enough to get it back."

My Daughter: "Did your parents sue the crib company?"

Me: "Nah. They just let me learn a Valuable Lesson. There was a lot of that going on back then."

My Son: "Didn't you ever get sick?"

Me: "No. We could drink straight from the garden hose or share a pop between four or five of us. In a glass bottle, no less. No harm done."

My Daughter: "Wow. What a life!"

Me: "No car seats, no sunscreen and every toy a certified choking hazard. It was pretty much heaven."

My Son: "Mom, I wish I was around when daddy was little."

My Wife: "Why? What's he been telling you this time?"

My Daughter: "Just about how he got to be so cool. Did you ever wonder?"

My Wife: "Honestly, that is one question I've never asked myself."

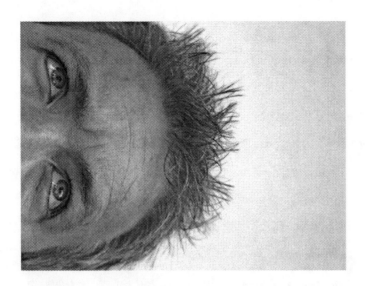

Parlez-vous Francais?

a lot of kids are complaining nowadays about having to study French in school. Let me just say this: Hey, this country IS bilingual (literally, "two linguals") and you had better get used to it. I support the teaching of an alternate language in our schools for two reasons.

Number One - It's good to be able to listen to the French version of CBC and see if they're getting more news than we are.

Number Two (and this is the biggest reason I support French in school) - I don't, personally, have to study it anymore. Now don't get me wrong. As a teenager, I paid my dues (in French, "mes pommes des terres"). I remember the long hours of lessons with Whipper Watson, memorizing details, reading endless chapters studying the Fathers of Confederation....

140

Well, maybe that was history, but no matter. I got through it and so will "vous."

Once you become as fluent as I am in both official languages (French and slang), the world will open its doors and you'll gain incredible understanding. You'll finally see well-worn terms in a new light. You'll see that there is no hunting season for a chocolate mousse; that the "RSVP" on an invitation actually stands for "Respond to Sylvio Plait" and that hors d'oeuvres have nothing to do with horses whatsoever. Yes, learning languages develops the mind. Several countries noted for more than one language have also made their mark in history: Germany - most citizens speak two or three languages AND this was the country that started both World Wars!

Switzerland - everybody speaks at least six languages (not counting Esperanto) and they invented the only cheese in the world with holes in it. If you get it going fast enough, it whistles.

In the short term, of course, it may seem useless to learn the language of "La Belle Province". I assure you that in the end, the work is worth it. Languages let you peer into the living rooms (les salles du bains) of other cultures. I have been out of high school for more than thirteen years. In that time I have experienced the "haute couture" (literally: hot cupboard) due, in part, to my fine education. My life has a certain "je ne sais pour quoi".

I firmly believe that education begins in the home or "dans le camion." Every day contains lessons that will prepare my children for living in this country.

"Son," I say, "someday you will go on a French Exchange and meet a beautiful French girl (a "bonnie lassie") and you will need to introduce yourself. Here is how I did it when I was your age: 'Bonjour, je m'appelle Mark. Je suis une chapeau du fromage.' (Hi, my name is Mark. Do you find me attractive?)

"If memory serves me correctly, she'll probably reply: 'Vous etes un idiot?' (Meaning: Are you single?)

"The reply should be something like: 'Oui, oui, je suis un tres petit dindon.' (Yes, yes, I am very lonely.)

"Mastering the French language will definitely set you apart from the others."

In fact, they might avoid you all together.

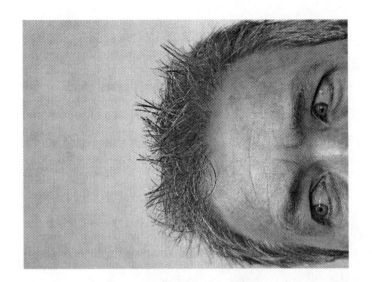

The Guinea Pigs

Sometimes it's good to have friends around who can help you avoid trouble, or at the very least, help you through it.

The 'trouble' started with my children's desire to get a pet. I was not against the idea. There are many potential pets that would work well in our house: Hermit Crabs, for example, and also various types of rock. In fact, if the pet can be contained within a…well, a container, then I don't have a problem with it. Look at how peacefully goldfish have lived among us!

I would not, however, be talked into getting a dog.

Why, you ask? Oh, my family tried to convince me. They made the promises of perpetual care and no responsibilities for dad. But I can see the future. I see our cute little puppy. I see our children playing with him all day. I see us feeding him and cleaning up after him until it's time to go to bed. And then what do I see? I see Mr. Cute Puppy yelping his cute little heart out 'til dawn's early light. I see neighbours plotting my untimely demise. I can also see Mr. Cute Puppy being Mr. I Want Some Exercise Half Way Through The Night. I know their mother won't let me push the kids out the door at 3am and she won't be raring to go herself, SO GUESS WHO GETS ELECTED!! And as all of you fathers know, if you do it once, you've just inherited a job!

This brings us to The Guinea Pigs. One day last month, I came across an obstacle in this pet dilemma that was too huge to overcome. It was insurmountable. A weapon too powerful to conquer. The "Death Star" of events. Thirty days ago, I was hit with: "The Cousin Who Got a Guinea Pig!!" That's right. There is no levy that can stop the tidal wave of "Jake has one! Can we get one?" AND "Honey, my sister says they are SO cute and easy to care for!" Being an expert in family dynamics, I knew I would lose this battle so, to cut my losses, I tried to find a way to make it more palatable. This meant a visit with my mentor, Luc. If anyone could help me through this hard time, it would be him.

Me: "I figure, a cage is mostly just an aquarium with holes. How much trouble can they be?"

Luc: "Exactly."

Me: "And the lady said as long as they're raised together, they won't fight, so that's good."

Luc: "Exactly."

Me: "And we got a cage for free so I know we're not going to be spending a lot of money on them, so that's a plus."

Luc: "Exactly."

Me: "You're right. We should just go ahead and get them."

One week later, we met again.

Luc: "Well, how is the extended family doing?"

Me: "What, you mean the Guinea Hogs? It ain't the best."

Luc: "But I thought they were raised together…"

Me: "Yeah, but they're also males. Two males don't get along so well. A male and a female get along TOO well. The best choice is two females."

Luc: "Well, at least they can't fight throughout the house. I mean, they are contained in the cage, right?"

Me: "Technically, THEY are. However, Guinea Pig fights consist of kicking sawdust at each other ninja-style and now it's all over the carpet."

Luc: "Well, that's not so…"

Me: "Five pounds of poopy, urine-soaked sawdust sitting on our new carpet."

Luc: "Well, um…hey, look at the money you saved with the new cage!"

146

Me: "I didn't get out of "Stupendous Pet" for under sixty bucks."

Luc: "Hey honey, the Guinea Pig idea worked!"

Me: "What are you talking about? I'm telling you these pets are a mistake!"

Luc: "I'm not talking about the animals. We were considering it too, but decided to let you go first and see what your experience was like. Sometimes it's good to have friends around that you can count on to help you avoid trouble."

Me: "I'm glad we could be your Guinea Pigs."

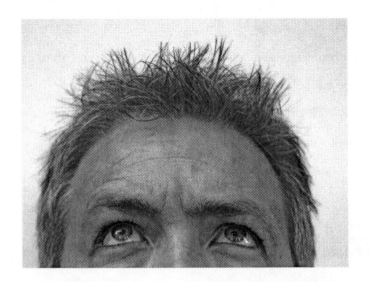

Being A
Superhusband

Okay, this is just a warning before you start reading. There may or may not be some mush in the following column. And, like traces of peanuts, you may or may not feel safe and comfortable with that. I know I don't.

On Saturday, our whole family went to the theatre to see "The Incredibles." In case you haven't heard, this is an animated feature about a Superhero Family. It was quite entertaining and well worth the week's pay I shelled out to see it on the big screen. The "gist" (pronounced: gist) of the movie is this: Mr. Incredible was this fantastic Superguy who was quite popular.

He marries this female Superperson and "settles down." Then Super-heroing is outlawed and his life REALLY starts to suck. First of all, he can't be a Superguy anymore. He has to get a "real" job. Then he starts putting on weight. Then his job falls apart (especially right after he punches his boss through the wall). Then we see him sneaking out of the house to do Super-things secretly.

I know this is going to sound crazy, but that whole part of the movie really struck a chord with me (whatever that means). You see I believe waaaay down in my heart that I am a kind of low-level superhero. Or at least, I was at one time. And it's not just me; EVERY man on the planet feels this way (about himself).

Example: When a guy straps a mattress to the roof of his car, he will also stick his arm out the window to hold it down. He truly believes that HIS ARM is somehow going to save the day if a gust of wind SNAPS the ropes he's using to hold down the mattress.

In the same way, we all get the feeling that being a Responsible Family Man has somehow DRAINED our superpowers from the core of our being. Isn't THAT great news for our wives! "Hello my Kryptonite-laden lover! I'm slowly dying because of you–but don't let it get you down!"

I guess for me it all comes down to expectations. When I got married, I didn't expect to have every single evening taken up by family things and every single night to be interrupted by one of the children waking up. I didn't expect that my great job wouldn't pay for all the bills we have every month.

I didn't expect that I would ever be the owner of a minivan.

I didn't expect that I would get love handles so soon.

I didn't expect those love handles to extend all the way around. I didn't expect so much hair to grow on my back and shoulders. (The back I don't mind so much because I don't have to see it, but the shoulders...) I didn't expect to be so TIRED all of the time. I bet Superman never had to deal with any of this stuff. I was revelling in self-pity when my son asked me a question.

My Son: "Dad, what did you want to be when you grew up?"

Me: "Well, I guess I wanted to be someone important. You know, someone that people looked up to."

My Son: "WOW! And you got your wish!! Can we wrestle now?" Maybe if I want to be a Superhero, I just have to set my sights a little lower. About two feet lower.

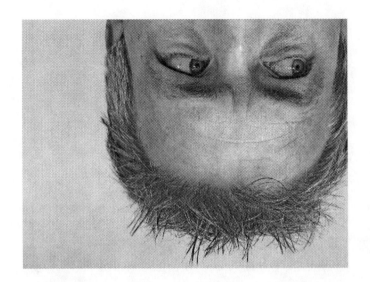

Maxims for Parenting

Some friends of mine just announced that they are Expecting. This is good because I can finally stop feeling sorry for myself and start laughing at someone else. I know that they have lots of questions. I also know that no matter what answers they get, nothing will sink in or make sense until they go through it all themselves. That's the hazard of being a first-time parent. On the plus side, the rest of us "experienced parents" get to stand on the sidelines and watch. It's good for a chuckle or two and it also reminds us of how far we've come and that there's hope for everybody. I now present, for your enjoyment and reference, a valuable aid for first-time parents:

LIFE 101'S MAXIMS FOR PARENTING

1. Nothing makes you want to punch somebody more than when they tell you that ALL babies sleep through the night.

2. As long as you are sitting on the edge of the bed in your underwear, the baby will go back to sleep.

As soon as you get under the blankets, he'll wake up again.

3. The day you scrub the floors is the same day that the baby will throw his bowl of food off the highchair.

4. You don't care where the soother has been. Stick it in your mouth and it will be clean.

5. Screaming infants are the only group in the world with whom you cannot negotiate.

6. You DID NOT just say to your children exactly what your parents said to you as a child. Even if what you said may have sounded A BIT like what your parents always told you, it was WAY different.

7. Your child's behavior at a social gathering will vary inversely with your chances for slipping quietly away. If you can leave at any time, he will be an angel. If you are in the front pew and the bride is coming down the aisle, he will be a spastic howler monkey.

8. The odds of your child sleeping through the night will increase dramatically when that child is at your mother's house. The more times you have complained to her about how terribly your baby sleeps, the more likely that child is to prove you wrong.

9. The music collection that your children will make fun of when they are older represents the last cool things you were able to buy before you started investing heavily in PAMPERS.

10. Portable phones, remotes and soothers all disappear at the most inopportune times.

11. Colic is God's way of punishing you for everything you did in college.

12. The greater your hurry, the greater the chance of having to change a diaper.

ADDENDUM: The more expensive your outfit, the more likely you are to get peed on.

13. There is no alarm clock in the world as effective as the sound of a child throwing up.

14. By the time child #2 shows up, you won't be sterilizing ANYTHING.

And so, Randy and Karen and whoever else may need this advice, clip these maxims out and put them on your fridge. Check each one off as you experience it. They may not help right away but they will remind you that we've all been to where you are going. It's a long, bumpy ride but we wouldn't have missed it for the world!

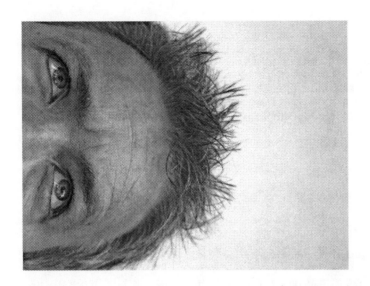

Central Air Conditioning

the secret to Marital Bliss, and I'm sure you'll back me up on this, is Central Air Conditioning. In fact, if you are married and living in a house without Central Air Conditioning, you may as well pack up your bags right now, because surely there must be SOMEONE ELSE out there who knows how to treat a woman right and give her the luxury she deserves.

Now, you have to give my wife credit (lots and lots of credit). She married a guy (me) who grew up WITHOUT CENTRAL AIR CON-DITIONING. In fact, when I grew up I lived in a farm house which actually takes the outside temperature, MAGNIFIES IT A THOUSAND TIMES and contains it under the roof for twenty-four hours (scientists have studied this). Being industrious, farming -type people, we developed a strategy called: Plunking A Big Fan On The Floor And Having All The Kids Sleep In Front Of It. This not only cooled us down, it also helped us to discover many fascinating things, not the least of which were the "Steam Roller" and how to make a robot voice by talking through the fan blades. Come to think of it, the "Plunking" strategy belonged to the kids. Our parents had a separate strategy called "Sleeping Downstairs." Ours was more fun.

Getting married, then, was a bit of a learning curve for me AND my wife since our first house had no air conditioning. In fact, it seems like we spent more time trying to understand each other than we did...well, getting to know each other.

My Wife: "Honey, can you sleep?"

Me: "Huh? What?"

My Wife: "It's three a.m. Can you sleep?"

Me: "Is this one of those trick questions all the guys warned me about?"

My Wife: "I can't sleep. It's too hot."

Me: "Why don't you just take off your pyjamas?"

My Wife: "Look at me. I'm down to the bare minimum as it is."

Me: "Oh, yes."

My Wife: "What can we do about this?"

Me: "Well, 'Seize The Day' comes to mind."

My Wife: "Don't even THINK about touching me."

Needless to say, I was motivated to become a Problem Solver. The way that I solved that particular problem was to move to a different house. One that had Central Air Conditioning. Things went well until one summer, out of the shimmering blue, it quit. Then it worked. Then it quit. This presented us with our biggest trial yet: did we spend our hard-earned money on a "Luxury Item" or did we limp along with what we had, thankful for the many days of enjoyment we had ALREADY experienced? I put my communication skills to work.

Me: "But, Honeycakes, we hardly ever have a problem with it."

My Wife: "There is something wrong with the Central Air and it must be fixed or replaced."

Me: "But Dearest, it works fine most of the time."

My Wife: "We live in Canada. We only have it ON for two months of the year."

Me: "I prefer to look at it as being problem-free for a solid ten months."

My Wife: "I will say this once. I am pregnant. There is no way that I am going through a summer without Central Air Conditioning."

I still had some good points to make, but because I loved her so much, I decided instead to make a few phone calls.

158

My Wife: "Thank you for buying new Central Air. It sure cooled things off in here."

Me: "Y-y-yeah, n-no p-problem. I'll s-see you in bed."

My Wife: "Sure, honey, you rascal, you."

Me: "No, I'm serious, I'm g-going to bed. I think I'm c-catching a cold."

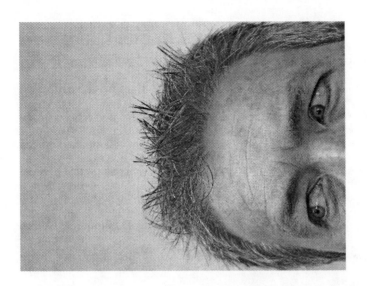

Convenient Financing

to 'Serve Me Better', a lot of things have gotten way less convenient. Instead of going into a bank and talking to one of ten bank tellers, I am now encouraged to burn gasoline as I wait patiently in the Drive-Thru to use the ATM. Luckily, banks have come up with an even easier way to Serve Me Better, namely telephone banking which is extremely convenient for me because I let my wife do it.

" Time to do some convenient telephone banking, honey!" I say on my way to bed. "Don't stay up too late!"

I must say that we are actually very happy with our banking institution. This is mostly because when we call them, the first thing they say to us is, "Thank you for being a customer!" You heard me right. The bank thanks ME for being a customer. I have to admit, when it first happened, it threw me for a loop. I mean, what is the world coming to when a bank goes off

160

and thanks a guy for being a customer? What's next? Loans below Prime? Anyway, as nice as they are, I think that the reason telephone banking is really being pushed is because when they are talking to you face-to-face and telling you about all of the things you can't do and all of the service charges they will apply when you do the things you need to do, it must be hard to keep a straight face. However, on the other end of a telephone line, a fellow may be in hysterics over your plight and you would never know it. The only way to be sure is to ask pointed questions and listen closely to the response.

EXAMPLE:

You: "So what you are telling me is that you are going to charge me for putting money INTO your bank..."

Telebanker: "Yes."

You: "And while it's in there, you are going to charge me to keep it there..."

Telebanker: "(ahem) Yes."

You: "And while it's in there, you are going to lend it out to other people..."

Telebanker: "(hee hee) Yes."

You: "And charge THEM money for using it..."

Telebanker: "(snicker) Yes."

You: "And when I close the account, you charge me for that too."

Telebanker: "(snort/snicker/heeheehee) Ahem. Yes. That's about the size of it. Thanks for being a customer."

Besides their good-natured sense of humor, telebankers are also great for recommending things to you. When we first opened our account, we did not realize how much we needed a Line of Credit. Thankfully, they did.

Telebanker: "Mr. Thrice, thank you for being a customer. Is there anything I can help you wi...WHOA! I see you don't have a line of credit yet."

Me: "No. I don't need one."

Telebanker: "HA! Of course you do. You own a house. You have children. You need a line of credit. Why risk it? We'll start you out at Five Thousand."

Me: "Risk it? Umm, sure. Five thousand sounds good."

(One week later)

Telebanker: "Mr. Thrice, thank you for being a customer. I see that you only have (haha) a five thousand dollar line of credit. I'll increase that to twenty for you. Anything else?"

Me: "Well, I'd like a car loan."

Telebanker: "Impossible. Your line of credit is way too high for that."

Me: "Boy, that line of credit sure is convenient."

162

Telebanker: "Anything to help!"

Me: "But that didn't help me."

Telebanker: "I wasn't referring to you."

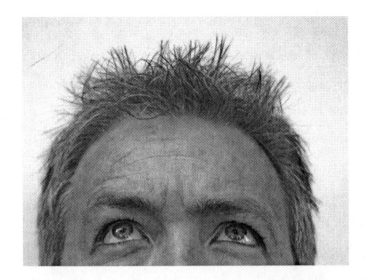

2001 SPACE DENTISTRY

there are certain advantages to having a sister-in-law who is a dental hygienist. You get free sermons on the value of fluoride and all your Christmas gifts come wrapped in floss. Every once in a while you may notice her taking particular interest in your smile, which inevitably means you are about to hear, "You should come in and get that looked at."

Nothing strikes fear in the heart of a man like those nine words.

I chipped my tooth. It didn't bother me that it was chipped. In fact, no one, including the person who cleaned my teeth, even noticed.

"Mark, for the last time, I CAN'T CLEAN YOUR TEETH IF YOU DON'T GET YOUR TONGUE OUT OF THE WAY!"

164

When she finally DID notice, however, I knew that I was in trouble. Relative or no, she was going to snitch. That meant that I had to make Another Appointment.

Here's a handy tip about the Dentist's Office: things are not what they seem. In fact, when you enter the office, you will notice the Relaxing Music playing softly in the background. Everyone smiles at you. The chairs are all VERY comfortable. Everybody wants to help YOU. It's hard to imagine that behind those pastel doors are the same devices used by Darth Vader as instruments of torture. So remember to keep your guard up and, if at all possible, your mouth closed.

Even though I had never met this Dentist before, my Appointment started off well. In fact, he was waiting for me at the front door. From there, however, things went downhill fast.

Dr. X: "Come on in, Mark. Let's have a look."

Me: "Sure, Doc. By the way, how long have you been practicing dentistry?"

Dr. X: "Since yesterday. HAHAHAHAHAHA! Only joking! I've been a Dentist for about eight months. Open wide."

Me: "(MONTHS? MONTHS? HE'S ONLY BEEN A DENTIST FOR 'MONTHS'?)"

Dr. X: "Alright, Mark. This will be a simple procedure and relatively painless."

Me: "Whew."

Dr. X: "We are going to do a Level 4 Veneer Prep..."

Me: "Oh. A Level 4 Veneer Prep. So we're bypassing Levels One to Three altogether."

Dr. X: "Exactly."

Me: "(Somebody should tell this guy that 'simple procedures' don't go by the name of 'Level 4 Veneer Prep.')"

Dr. X: "...then we are going to Bevel the tooth."

Me: "(BEVEL THE TOOTH? TEETH DON'T GET BEVELLED! WOOD GETS BEVELLED. I DON'T WANT A BEVELLED TOOTH! THIS GUY IS A LOON.)"

It was about that time that I noticed the television on the ceiling. "Maybe this guy isn't so bad after all," I thought, and began to relax. Then he brought out the cotton swab and started rubbing it on my gum. Those of you who have been to the Dentist know that should have been fair warning.

Dr. X: "Now I'm just applying some topical aesthetic."

Me (watching monkeys cavort on TV): "Uh huh."

Dr. X: "You may feel some slight discomfort..."

Me (watching monkeys bathe themselves): "Uh huh."

166

Dr. X (Pulling out a 6- inch long needle): "There will be a small pinch..."

Me (watching monkeys hurl nuts at each other): "AAAAAAGH! WHAT WAS THAT? SOMEBODY STUCK A NEEDLE IN MY HEAD! SIMPLE PROCEDURES DON'T HAVE NEEDLES STICKING INTO MY HEAD! IS THIS SOME KIND OF JOKE?"

Dr. X: "There. Now we can get to work."

And for the next 45 minutes, he worked away at my Level 4 while I developed the condition known as 'Hippo Mouth'. My teeth, lips, gums and most of my nasal cavity were frozen and slowly ballooning to the size of a jumbo hippopotamus.

Dr. X: "Well Mark, that's it. We're done. Unless you want us to keep going with your other teeth. HAHAHA."

Me: "HA HA (Drool)"

My sister-in-law: "Here, Mark, I'm sending you home with a little souvenir...a new toothbrush!"

Me: "Great. What have you got in the shape of a hippo or monkey?"

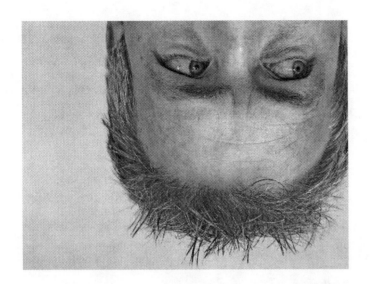

There Goes the Neighborhood

it is time once again for famed advice columnist Dr. Bigbrain to be our guest. The theme for today's column is Working Outdoors.

Dear Dr. Bigbrain,

Can you help me? The new guy down the street keeps coming over and asking me for advice on how to garden. It's kind of bothersome but I feel sorry for him. What should I do?

Hot and Bothered

Dear Hot,

I understand your frustration. The problem is that everybody is good at something and no good at something else. In our neighborhood, for instance, everybody knows that they can come to me for pearls of wisdom about life and love and I have no reservations whatsoever about getting help from them when it comes to odd jobs around the house.

Dear Dr. Bigbrain,

I need help, too. My neighbor two doors down borrowed my ladder, my lawn mower and my garden hose right after he moved in two months ago. How do I ask for them back?

Taken Advantage Of

Dear Taken,

Here is a piece of timely advice that you can take to the bank: tools don't last forever- friends do! So what if somebody borrowed a few tools! That is nothing compared to the solid relationships you will be developing with those around you. I can honestly tell you that I personally have NO IDEA whose tools are whose in my own garage. And I don't care! What I do care about is feeling the love.

Dear Dr. Bigbrain,

It seems like every house on our street looks great with the exception of one. This new guy moved in a few months ago and has yet to even mow his lawn. I know that the problem is not from the lack of tools because he's borrowed something from everyone in the neighborhood! Maybe if he spent more time working and less time dispensing his "Pearls of Wisdom" to anything with a pulse he might actually get something done for a change. Is there any way to get it through this guy's incredibly THICK SKULL that the rest of the world will keep on spinning even without his brain droppings but if he doesn't return EVERY SINGLE THING THAT HE'S BORROWED AND START TO WORK ON HIS YARD, WE WILL HUNT HIM DOWN LIKE THE DOG THAT HE IS AND COMPOST HIS REMAINS?

Head of the Village Mob

Dear Head,

You know, it's funny that you say that. You see, in OUR neighborhood, I'm the new guy. Yes, I've borrowed a few tools. No, I haven't had time to really do much with my lawn since, oh gosh, April. But the guys on my street just joke about it. "Hey Tarzan," they say, "how about cleaning up that mess you call a yard and restoring our property values back to what they were before you moved in." And they REALLY look serious! What a bunch of kidders!

Dear Dr. Bigbrain,

My husband refuses to do ANY work on our house. All he does is talk to the neighbors and take their stuff. I haven't seen the sidewalk in days. Now none of the neighbors are talking to us. One of them loaded the back seat of the car with manure to get his attention. It didn't work. Help.

Worried Wife

170

Dear wife,

This whole situation sounds familiar. In fact, I think I even recognize your hand writing. Wait a minute. IS THIS MY WIFE? ARE YOU ALL WRITING ABOUT ME?

YOU CAN SAY GOODBYE TO GETTING THE LAWN MOWED TONIGHT (although this does explain the funny smell in the car this morning). AND TELL OUR STUPID NEIGHBORS THAT THEY'LL SEE THEIR TOOLS AGAIN, AT THE NEXT YARD SALE!!

Honestly, I hate people. That's why I got into writing.

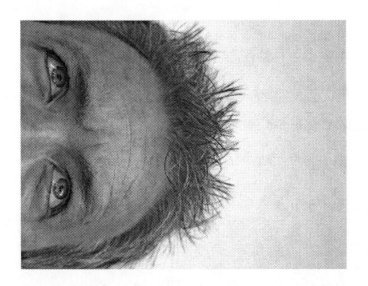

Diary of a
Pregnant Husband

the problem with being married to a woman who is eight months pregnant is that she is forever uncomfortable and it is your fault. Her basic goal at this point in life is to find THE PERFECT SPOT or position in which to stand, sit or lie.

You will notice this most when she is sleeping. Please read that last sentence over again very slowly. YOU will notice this most when SHE is sleeping. The reason that you will notice anything is that you are NOT sleeping. Don't get me wrong. You want to sleep. Oh, do you want to sleep. This is impossible, however, because a certain anonymous mate of yours (who will remain nameless) (and pregnant) spends the night 'shifting.'

Now let's be honest here. Everyone's gotta shift sometimes. But most people (myself included) opt for a nice, quiet shift. Not the kind that

172

displaces your partner. The expectant mother, however, has bulldozer shifting down to a science:

Stretch (WiggleWiggle) Shift

Shift (Sigh) Shift Roll

Roll Shift Roll (Belch) Roll

Snore

Finally, at about four a.m., you sense that she has stopped moving. She may or may not be dead; you don't care. In fact, she is cuddled up beside you and sleeping peacefully. It takes a few minutes before you realize exactly how she has achieved her comfort: she is lying with her head on your arm and has thrown her leg over you, pinning you down. Unfortunately for you, her leg happens to be resting on your bladder which, over the last five hours, has slowly filled to its limit. The normal response would be to climb out of bed and relieve yourself but you can't because SHE HAS FOUND THE PERFECT SPOT and she is not moving for ANYBODY. And besides, all of the blood has drained out of your arm and you couldn't get up if your life depended on it.

So you decide to wet the bed, which actually works out well because, suddenly, she's up off of you and muttering something about "doing more Kegels."

The rest of the night is spent comforting your children as they are intermittently woken up. "No, that's not a monster," you say reassuringly. "Mommy's just sleeping 'loudly.'"

Besides the 'comfort' thing, another phenomenon to be wary of is "Nesting." This is where the Paranoia Fairy visits your wife and tells her that if the baby was born RIGHT NOW, during Oprah, she would have to sleep in a crate in the basement until the Children's Aid came to pick her up. Somehow this means that YOU must immediately go outside and paint the garage door. Upon completing that task, you will be given another and another until you are spending more time working ON the house than you are actually living IN the house. Your other children refer to you as "The Custodian" and you find yourself fantasizing about the baby's arrival for the sole reason that your wife will finally have someone else to pick on.

Then a buddy from your office says something like, "Wow, eight months already! That was fast!" And you punch him in the bladder.

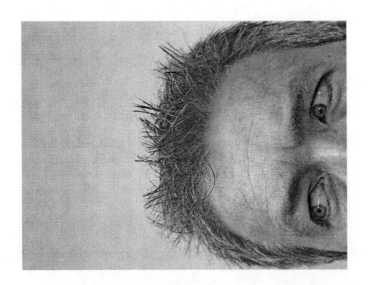

Smart Parenting
for Guys

"the baby is eating his Goldfish crackers off the ground."

If this statement had been made eight years ago, I, as a new father, would have scooped the baby up, whisked him into the house and washed out his mouth. My wife would have been on the phone, having a harried conversation with her mother: "He's just eaten dirt!" "What kind of dirt? Do you have a cat?"

As it is, I am not a new father. I am an old father and that means that I don't run ANYWHERE. It means that our third and final child is bound to develop a lot of "character" and that everything that happens to him will be "good for him". You may be sitting there thinking that I am a terrible parent but I can tell you that, after years of painstaking research, I don't care.

176

You see, I know the secret to parenting, or more specifically, FATHERING. That is: Don't sweat it.

Of course, in the eyes of our nine-year-old neighbor, Celine, I am probably the worst father she has ever seen. Because she doesn't have a little brother in her own family, Celine doesn't understand that they put everything in their mouths, including house pets and furniture. It is not uncommon for the little guy to be playing in the sand box and gulping back sand like a fish swallows water. Traditionally, we have been against this, mostly because he looks to be enjoying himself and as parents we cannot allow that to continue. However, how does one prevent a child from eating dirt? Play with him 24/7? Not convenient. Apply duct tape? Not allowed. So my plan is to relax and get creative. In my defence, I'd like to say that I don't think she's had ANY kids herself and so our third child is Celine's first baby experience. Therefore when she says to me (with a notable tone of alarm), "The baby is eating his Goldfish crackers off the ground," I am inclined to stay in my hammock and not react swiftly (or at all) in the hopes that when she grows up and gets married, she'll remember these lessons and never ask me to baby-sit her kids. The chances of this happening increase with each of her visits.

The real conflict here is between me and Celine's nurturing instinct. I think that I will win. Not because I am stronger, mind you, but because her nine-year-old nurture is nowhere near the level of my wife's. If I can handle my wife, I can handle Celine. (By "handle my wife," I mean "do what I want outside when she's in the house.") You may not understand the importance of this classic struggle. In literary circles, they say that the crises of any story centre on Man vs Man, Man vs Nature or Man vs Himself. In real life, the crises go from Man vs His Hormones to Man vs His Wife's Hormones, then finally conclude at Man All By Himself. These female hormones are what we as men seek to understand and manipulate for they power the Nurturing Instinct, as well as other instincts (The Cleaning Up Instinct and The 'Does This Skirt Make Me Look Fat' Instinct to name a few).

My point here is that even though my neighbor is only nine years old and about a million years away from getting married and starting a family, I can still help out her future husband by showing her my parenting skills. No, I don't come running when he eats dirt. That's okay because I put Goldfish crackers IN the dirt so at least he will be getting SOME form of nutrition. This makes sense. At least now he's getting his Recommended Daily Allowance of something. If toymakers really knew what they were doing, they'd find a way to take all of their toys for toddlers and coat them in vitamins. Let's face it; the toys are going into the mouth as soon as they're out of the box. Why not take advantage of this natural behavior? Instead of NEW AND IMPROVED on the packaging, we'd see A GREAT SOURCE OF VITAMIN C!

Through my focused efforts, I hope that someday Celine will be able to see exactly what kind of people we guys are. And by that I mean the resourceful, trustworthy kinds who are consumed with finding different, nay BETTER, ways of parenting that ensure we can spend more time in the hammock.

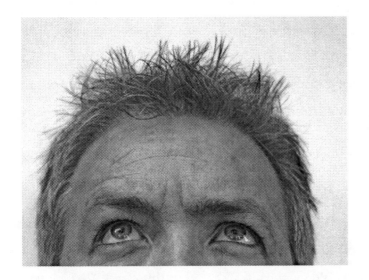

Happy Father's Day

most people that I know don't like going to see the doctor. It may be the long wait in the waiting room; it may be that their particular doctor is not that helpful or that nice. In my case, our family doctor, Doctor Joe, is both knowledgeable and accommodating. I can talk to him about almost anything and trust that his advice will be that of an experienced friend. In the same sense, I don't call him very often because I find that there are very few things happening to me that a good night's sleep, lots of fluid and a few new comic books can't cure. The exceptions include things requiring a prescription and a plantar wart from the devil himself.

About two weeks ago, I started feeling tender in my stomach area. My lower stomach. In fact, it was such a low part of my stomach that some, including those with even a minimal knowledge of the human body, could refer to it in technical terms as my "personal area." And so, like every other reasonable man in the new millennium, I wanted to get to the bottom of it. I wanted to find out what was going on with my body and I was willing to go to any lengths to do it, just as long as I didn't have to tell anyone else or go through some sort of silly examination. This pretty much eliminated all choices except the traditional G.B.I.B.G. option so popular with my father's generation. Yes, the Grin, Bear it and Be Grumpy method was always a hit at our house when dad's back went out and I knew it would be equally accepted in this case: "Why are you so grumpy? Why don't you go mow the lawn or something?"

I had a funny feeling that something had to be done. Actually, it was because I had the 'funny feeling' that I knew that something had to be done. It was a simple conversation with my daughter that really moved me to act.

"Daddy, I'm your sweetheart." That's all she said. Then she wrapped her chubby little arms around my neck and squeezed like there was no tomorrow. There had to be a tomorrow. A thousand tomorrows for this little girl and her daddy. Alright, alright, I'll make the appointment already.

Now, even though I like Doctor Joe and I COMPLETELY trust Doctor Joe, I must admit I was quite hesitant about explaining my problem to the good man and letting him do his thing, so to speak. Perhaps, I thought, I should just go to EMERG and let some stranger handle the problem. That idea had barely formed when it was quickly replaced with visions of STUDENT DOCTORS (male OR female) throwing back the curtain and opening up their First Year Biology Book. "Geez, I dunno. Maybe someone else should take a crack at this."

"So, how can I help you?" asked the good Doctor.

Me: "Well, Doc, it's like this. We both have a problem today."

Dr. Joe: "We do?"

Me: "Yeah. My problem is that I'm sore in my "speedo" area and yours is that you're my doctor and you have to help me."

Dr. Joe: "Okay, okay. No problem. Let's have a look."

Just for the record, that means "Stand here in your birthday suit while I perform a THOROUGH examination." I don't think I've ever been as... tense as I was for that brief period.

Me: "...So...how are you?"

Dr. Joe: "Fine. Does this hurt? How about this? This?"

Me: "No...No...AAAAGHH!"

Dr. Joe: "Ah. You've got epididimitis. It's a type of inflammation."

Me: "You mean it's not cancer? Doc, I could kiss you!"

Dr. Joe: "How about you just put your pants on."

One prescription of tetracycline and a bottle of pain relievers later and I'm good to go. I would gladly trade 15 minutes of embarrassment for the chance to continue being someone's sweetheart.

Happy Father's Day to me.

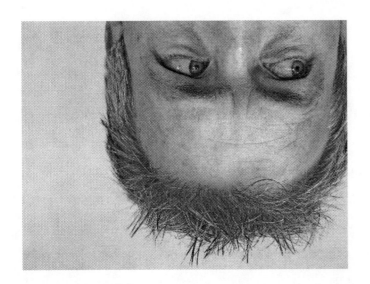

Babies for Dummies

Okay, so for nine months you look forward to the time when everything will be back to "normal" (meaning, of course, your wife will at least look at you without grinding her teeth and wincing). Then the great day arrives and the baby is born. As prepared as you are for your wife to throw herself at you in a wave of passion, you find that instead, she is throwing all of her energy into the silly, inexplicable things that mothers do such as feeding the baby, burping the baby and cleaning herself off.

So what you need is some way to come alongside her, enter into her baby world, share her joys and frustrations and hopefully get some attention along the way. When you show her that you are an expert at handling infants, you free her up to do what she REALLY wants to do: pounce on you! Sound difficult? Take heart, oh husband. All is not lost.

184

With a few Life 101 tips under your belt, you should soon be on the express road to Smooch City.

BABY HANDLING FOR DUMMIES (Yes, this means YOU)

To cut right to the chase, the time where you will shine most as an expert is when you help put your baby to bed.

"Here, I'll take him to his crib," you must offer in your most cheerful, manly voice. After all, you think to yourself, he already appears to be unconscious and once he's in bed, you no longer have to share your wife.

You will note that the journey TO the nursery is relatively uneventful. The tot will remain curled up in your arms with the usual frown that all babies wear when they sleep. However, be careful. What you do next may mean the difference between a night of unbridled television watching and one where you stand outside the nursery door crying silently to yourself. You see, in some ways, babies are like explosives. They are unpredictable and are most dangerous when you try to move them. And this is precisely what you have to do: transfer the sleeping child FROM your arms TO his crib without disturbing him.

This is impossible.

I believe that babies, as you carry them close to your chest, can feel how your heart pounds as you approach your destination. They like this. They think it's funny. They know that once you reach the crib, there is no physical way you can reach OVER the side and DOWN to the mattress (usually a distance of about two metres) without breaking a rib or dropping your package.

However, you have to do it. Do it and know that within two minutes the child will be crying. (Most start right away. The really mean ones wait until you leave). So now you have a choice. You can choose to pick him up again and risk breaking another rib OR you can give him his soother.

Soothers (or pacifiers) are wonderful little inventions. The idea behind them is that they will offer some satisfaction and comfort when mom is not interested in providing either. The problem arises when you, standing in the pitch darkness, attempt to stick one into your screaming child's mouth. You will miss. It will go into his eye, his ear and his pudgy, little cheek but you will never hit his mouth, no matter how hard or rapidly you jab as you lean over the side of the crib. This will only serve to make Junior cry EVEN HARDER which is good because with his mouth open so wide, you have a bigger target!

Now the baby is starting to calm down and you turn the monitor back on so that your wife can hear what's happening. After you do that, take a look at your child and try to remember exactly HOW your wife told you to lay him down. On his back? On his side? On his tummy? Thankfully, there are a limited number of options or you would be there all night, not that that helps you right now. Right now you are trying to remember what your wife said as you left the room. What was it?

On his back!

NO! On his side!

As panic sets in, the only thing that you recall is her telling you that if you lay him down wrong, HE COULD DIE.

186

This does not help.

Fortunately for you, the monitor picks up whining fairly well and before you know it, your wife is behind you.

"Everything okay, honey? You've been up here for over an hour."

You: "Umm...yeah, I was just sticking around to, you know, make sure he was alright and maybe organize the diapers."

Your Wife: "I was hoping you would have come right back down. I wanted to cuddle. Oh well, it's time to feed him again. Do me a favour and get him out of the crib?"

You: "If my ribs don't break, I think my heart just might."

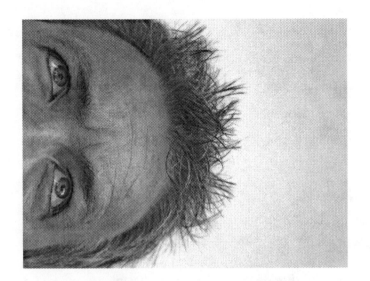

Baby Steps

the birth of your child is a wonderful event, full of wonder. Don't be fooled, however, into thinking that it's all milk and honey from that point on. (Although there does seem to be an overabundance of milk)(Coming from your honey)(HO!). Quite the opposite, there are a few things that you will need to be continually working on with both your child and spouse as the days go by.

#1 CLEARING THE AIR

Getting the baby to eat is not usually a problem. To ensure that the child in question eats as much as he can though, you must help him by making sure that his entire digestive system is absolutely clear of anything at all. The way to do this is to develop an abnormal fixation with burping and farting. And when I say "abnormal," I mean that you will find yourself congratulating your baby and each other for every noise that escapes his cheeks. Discontinue this practice before the child reaches puberty.

You want to make sure that at several points during his meal and immediately afterwards you quickly grab him, suspend him in various positions over your body and whack him vigorously. (This is one of those jobs where husbands can feel VERY useful). Almost any position is suitable for this, although there are a few traditional ones which work quite well:

OVER THE SHOULDER–Place the baby so that his tummy is on your chest and his head is on your shoulder. Lightly thump his bottom and lower back until he belches. Remember that when it was INSIDE, the gas was beneath a bellyful of milk. Since the gas has escaped, most likely the milk has, too. Have someone else clean up the mess.

Other popular burping positions include SITTING UP ON YOUR LAP (for puking on your crotch) and LAYING ACROSS YOUR LAP (for puking on the guy beside you).

When the baby is exceptionally gassy, you may want to coax it out the other end. To accomplish this, lay the baby on his back and fold his legs up to his chest. If that yields no results, have the husband encourage him by giving a demonstration.

#2 SLEEPING THROUGH THE NIGHT

Nothing can match the blissful slumber that you achieve when, for the first time in his life, your infant sleeps through the night. Oh the rapture!

Oh the tranquility! You wake up totally refreshed and relaxed with a whole new outlook on life.

This lasts for about twelve seconds. Then you realize that YOU HAVEN'T HEARD ANYTHING FROM YOUR BABY ALL NIGHT and run, screaming, into the Nursery to make sure that he's okay, waking him up in the process.

However, this feeling of terror pales in comparison to what your wife is going through at this very moment. She also has just realized that the baby has slept the whole night through and that the milk her body had produced for him four hours earlier HAS NOW TURNED INTO REALLY HARD CHEESE.

Husbands, take note here. No matter how you offer to help in this situation, you will not be appreciated, or even tolerated. Please, for your sake, just go get the baby, leave quietly and no one will be hurt.

When it's time to burp the baby, she'll call you. Use these moments to work on your technique.

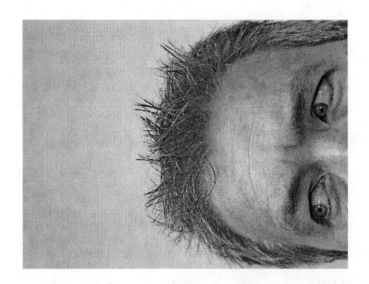

Birthday Party
Pay Back

birthday Party #5

The reason that you throw a birthday party for a 5-year-old is not so he can celebrate with his friends and get lots of presents. It is, in fact, to get revenge on all the parents whose kids invited your kids to THEIR birthday parties. A successful party can be measured in increments:

BRONZE LEVEL- kids come home excited about the games they've played, the food they ate and the presents they saw.

SILVER LEVEL- kids come home with loot bags full of candy and trinkets. It takes an half an hour to get the icing out of their hair. They already have a list of who is coming to THEIR party and what they're going to do.

192

GOLD LEVEL- kids come home babbling like howler monkeys. Every inch of their bodies is covered with dirt or some form of sticky syrup. They've had so much sugar that, even sitting still, they vibrate. You and your wife take turns with them as they spend the night throwing up.

When you first tell your child that he can have a party for his birthday and invite whomever he wants, you will discover an amazing truth about human nature. Namely that your child, at 5, has more friends now than you have accumulated over your 30 year life-span. So you need to find a way to trick him into only inviting as many kids as you think you can handle (ha!). Try something like: "Who are your three BEST friends in the whole world?" or "Well, since you are five, you get to have five friends over," or "Y'know, there's only one kid that I know of who actually likes you..."

Once the list is complete, you must be sure to know a little about each child who will be showing up. Important questions you may want to ask yourself include: How much food can this kid pack away? Is he allergic to anything I can be blamed for? If he falls off of the play centre, will he bounce?

It is paramount that you hold the party at a local park. Not only is the scenery beautiful and the equipment fun, you can be assured that no parent will be late in picking their kids up when you tell them that YOU are leaving the park at one o'clock.

What separates the Champion party-throwers from the Bronze medalists and the 'also-rans' is the food. What birthday would be complete without hotdogs? Someone should do a study on how many of those things a five year old can physically hold in his stomach because I know that with a little urging and some friendly competition, we were pretty much at capacity. The "piece de resistance" (literally: piece of cake), however, was dessert. Imagine being a kid and hearing: "Ok, everybody gets a cupcake. Put as much icing and as many gummy worms, chocolate sprinkles, sweet tarts and Smarties on them as you can and dig in." Heaven, right? You would think that the kids would bowl us over in a mad scramble for sweets but NO, in fact, I found myself offering, suggesting, even DEMANDING that they pile on as much confection as possible. This not only serves to make you quite popular with your guests, it will also help their parents to remember who you are as well.

You'll know you are a success when your child gets invited to one of THEIR parties. "Ben had such a GOOD time at your son's party. All night he was bringing up different things you did...we made a special note to remember to pay you back."

Diary of an Itchy Madman

the good news is that I'm irresistible to females. In fact, last week they were all over me! From the minute I rose from my bed to the second I lay down again, they would not leave me alone.

The bad news is that those females were mosquitoes .

Now, before you get out your computer and e-mail me your grandmother's recipe for a guaranteed mosquito repellent, let me say this: I've tried it all. Nothing works. I've tried Skin-So-Soft, garlic, Vitamin B1, DEET, not showering. Female mosquitoes find themselves helpless around me, regardless of the consequences.

As I mentioned last week, we go camping in the Muskokas every year. (Motto: We have rocks! And bugs!) Every year I grumble like an old curmudgeon about getting attacked by pesky insects and every year my wife pulls more "Repellent Ideas" off of the Internet, promising me that, "This year it will be different!" But it's never different. Every year is exactly the same: I slather myself with stinky goop. I get bitten. I ingest some concoction. I get bitten. I put the moves on my wife. She walks away.

This year, drawing on my vast experience with various mosquito repellents, I have developed my own formula which is GUARANTEED TO WORK. Here it is:

Take a whole bottle of Vitamin B1 tablets. Crush them in a mixing bowl. (Just the pills)

Add a half a cup of Skin- So- Soft.

Add a half a cup of Muskol.

Add a clove of garlic, diced.

Stir in a mixing bowl until the mixture is a thick paste.

Roll into a cylinder.

Bake at 350 Degrees for one hour.

When finished, you will have baked yourself a stinky little mosquito bat. Use it to club the little buggers.

The worst part of staying in mosquito country is watching your kids getting bitten. "Don't scratch!" you tell them. "If you ignore the bites, they'll go away." This, of course, is the stupidest thing to say to someone who is itchy, but as parents, saying stupid things is our right. The tables really turn when we get bitten ourselves, though. Like a fool, I tried to practice what I preached.

Saturday- Arrive at the cottage amidst a downpour. Luckily our "welcoming committee" isn't put off by a little weather. Got bitten six times. Should have put on repellent when I left the house seven hours ago.

Sunday- Rain has stopped, leaving everything soaking wet. Perfect weather for mosquitoes. Got another five bites. Have decided not to think about them and apply more of the goop my wife got off the 'net.

Monday- Sunny with a little breeze, so the mosquitoes are out in force. My ankles are now fairly covered with welts but only moderately itchy. Mind over matter really works!

Tuesday- Today we headed into town so I slipped on my sneakers. Who would have thought that would make my feet even itchier? I was so distracted I didn't notice the nine other bites I got on the back of my neck.

Wednesday- Kids are starting to get on my nerves with all their whining. "Just pretend you weren't even bitten," I yell. "Besides, I've got ten times as many bites as you. You don't see me complaining, do you?" My wife gives me a time out.

Thursday- Hot, hot, hot with no wind. You can hear them coming a mile away. Buzzing. Buzzing. They know who I am. They know where I

198

live. Even my sweat works against me, bringing my irritation to an exasperating crescendo. I gnaw on my fingers constantly. The children cling to their mother.

Friday- I spend the night fantasizing about sandpaper. I slap myself constantly, in case I'm being bitten and don't know it. Right before supper, I find myself purposely running into trees, just for the scrapes. Finally, at midnight, I give in to my primal urges and run my claws over my bites. "YES! YES! YES!" I holler. "Is there a problem?" my wife asks. I lay awake for the next four hours, quietly exulting in the pleasure of finger nails.

Saturday- Time to leave!! I start packing before the sun comes up. Plenty of mosquitoes out, but that's okay! I kind of like them now. HA HA HA. They are my friends. I love getting bitten. Welts are very soothing.

My Wife: "You look really itchy. Tell you what, when we get home I'll get on the "net" and download a remedy for those bites."

Me: "Yeah. HA HA HA HA. How about this? Don't bother."

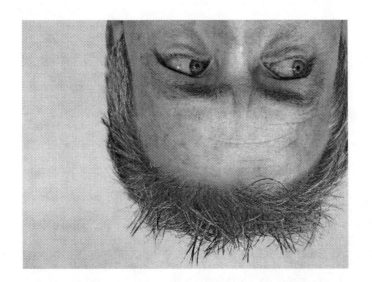

Expecting the Unexpected

a h, pregnancy! That beloved time when a visit from the stork leaves a woman positively glowing. And universally, who gets better treatment, even by total strangers, than someone who is "Expanding Her Girth For Birth." Like Moses on the Red Sea, she parts the crowds to make a path. Like the Queen, her very presence commands that you attend to her comfort. And woe be to the husband who ignores these commands.

The problem is that from the outside, pregnant people look so timid and docile...almost fragile. One has only to look to the husband, though, to see the OTHER side of conception.

The first thing that you must do is IDENTIFY the husband. Luckily, this does not prove to be too difficult. He is the one walking behind the pregnant person (usually carrying a plate of food) with an air of quiet desperation about him. You see, nobody told husbands what would happen when Mr. Stork visited. All they knew was that to GET Mr. Stork to visit, they had to be frisky. This seemed like a good deal. Now, realistically, they should have known that there would be a down-side. And really, their older, more experienced friends should have warned them. But that's just not how it works. All the "professional" moms love to watch the change from 'Confident Man Of The World' to 'Scared Rabbit.' And even though the professional dads want to step in with a word of warning, they're not allowed.

It seems like us guys struggle with women for most of their lives. We like them, yet when we get involved with them, we can't help feeling that we're in WAY over our heads, like trying to reel in a Great White Shark while on water-skis. Somehow though, we decide to marry. This brings us into unavoidable contact with the opposite sex on a regular basis. We weren't counting on that. Especially when they get moody. Despite that, the urge to start a family takes hold, introducing a whole new set of variables for the husband to be confused by, not the least of which is the concept of "Stretch Pants" (a cross between regular pants and a latex balloon). True, they make a statement. That statement is "Grandpa Walton." He knows it. She knows it. However when push comes to shove (and with a pregnant woman, I mean that literally), he will assure his wife that they are "really nice".

Laugh if you will, but you must realize what the husband in question understands completely: he is not dealing with the person he married.

Somehow (and he hasn't figured out how this happened), he is now dealing with someone whose weight is approaching his own. Someone who is awash in a cocktail of hormones (including more testosterone than he ever had). Someone who is given to snap mood swings. He treads lightly. This is why he does not complain when she hogs all the pillows in the house or cleans off her plate and then helps him with his. Lack of sleep and nutrition are small prices to pay for surviving what many (non-married) experts label "The Most Wonderful Stage Of Life."

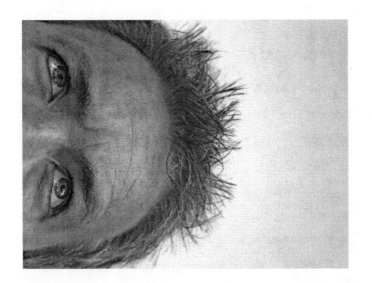

The Expecting Mother

Okay, okay. Let me start out by saying this: I had no idea how strongly some of you (pregnant) people felt about...well, being pregnant! So, in the interest of fair play (and for my own good health), I have decided to continue my series on pregnancy for one more week, this time utilizing some 'input' from several 'sources' to protect my "career."

I think the biggest point that I need to get across to everybody (ie. every other male in the known universe) is that while pregnancy MAY BE the most beautiful miracle in a human being's life, the fact remains that it still opens women up as targets for the most CRUEL jokes known to (ahem) man.

JOKE #1 THE ULTRASOUND

There are a lot of misconceptions about this whole process. First of all, let me explain something about the "picture." Nobody can see

ANYTHING in that picture. In fact, doctors use the same picture for EVERYBODY. But considering what women go through to GET that picture, you had better believe they can see their baby there. And if you know what's good for you, so will you. A good line that I always use is: "Oh my, what a cute little nose." I don't think God punishes people for humoring pregnant women.

SIDE NOTE: The picture that all the doctors give out is, in fact, an old satellite image of Hurricane Hazel. There may be some irony in this, after all.

Anyways, back to Joke #1. The reason that this joke works so well is that a pregnant woman's bladder is about the size of a small tea bag. (Whereas a normal woman's bladder is somewhere near the size of a bigger tea bag, with "wings.") Add to this the fact that for some unknown reason, the baby uses that "tea bag" as a footstool/trampoline and you begin to see the problem.

"Now in order to get a really good picture of your baby," the doctor says with a straight face, "you need to drink EIGHTEEN GLASSES OF WATER WITHOUT PEEING." So, wanting to be a good patient and knowing that if this is the third or fourth child, this may be the ONLY picture that gets taken until it graduates, the mom-to-be obediently gulps down her liquids. Then, she drives to the hospital where she waits in the Waiting Room for her name to be called. You have to understand that by now, the baby will have discovered that his 'Foot stool' just got overstuffed in a major way and HE IS GOING TO TRY IT OUT! That is why of all the Waiting Rooms to hang around in, the worst one is in the Ultrasound department with its gang of teeth-gritting, lip-biting, leg-crossing women who would as soon kill you as watch you finish your coke.

The joke has just begun. The funniest part is that when her name is finally called, she thinks that she is about to experience some relief. Little does she know that the process of completing an Ultrasound involves the "technician" grabbing a paperweight and pressing down on Mom's tea bag with all her might. For fifteen minutes.

Knowing that experienced moms will have the foresight to steel themselves for this appointment, doctors have recently extended the length of time for an Ultrasound to ONE SOLID HOUR. (Apparently their expressions are priceless!)

JOKE #2 NO MEDICATION

So there they are: tired, sore, emotional, crampy, hungry, tired and hungry (and emotional). AND when they get sick, they can't take anything stronger than vinegar. A cold that should last ten days now drags on for sixteen weeks. Expect their snores to approach the level of 'Congested Heifer.'

JOKE #3 WADDLING

YOU try standing around all day with a watermelon hanging down over your personal area. It's no wonder they have a top speed of three miles per day and walk like drunken penguins. Most men would be bed-ridden by the sixth month.

So there you have it. The cruellest jokes are played on the nicest people. With the smallest tea bags.

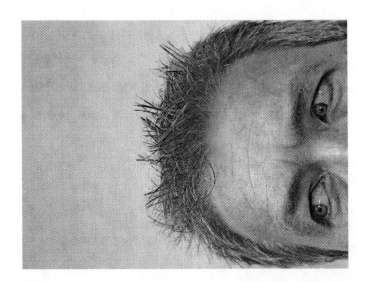

My Father's Day Letter

dear son,

Since it is Father's Day, I thought that I would write you a short letter to explain a few things. I know that as you get older, you will start to wonder: "What does it mean to be a Dad?" and "Is there some sort of training involved?" and "Why did MY Dad miss it?" Well, son, the truth is that there is much more to being a Dad than meets the eye. Even with me. What you may not realize is that I really have no idea of what I'm doing. No one does (never tell your mother this). When I look back at the day "we" decided to start a family, (when you are older and dating, you will come to know the meaning of "we"), I can honestly say that I was pretty clueless. Plus, and you will notice this by looking at our wedding pictures, I must have been about fourteen. Somehow I have survived as a father, proof of which is the fact that YOU have survived as a child. This means that I have either learned something, or I have been incredibly lucky. I will now share with you the Secrets Of Fatherhood, as far as I know them at this moment.

Rule #1- Speak With Confidence. As a father, it will be your duty to answer ALL SORTS OF QUESTIONS. The most important thing is to give an answer right away. Do not panic. Your answers do not have to be one hundred per cent accurate or even truthful, for that matter. (This rule applies when answering questions from your wife as well as your children)

EXAMPLE:

Your Wife: "Honey, we've been driving around for hours. Are you sure you know where we are going?"

You (raising your eyebrows and smiling):"Yeah, the road we're ON runs parallel to the one we WANT, but its,um, faster. I'm just looking for the right intersection..."

EXAMPLE #2:

Your Kid: "Daddy, what makes our van go?"

NOTE: Questions like this have a great potential for detail and confusion and will make your mother cringe.

You: "Remember how the van won't go unless I put the KEY into it?"

Your Kid: "Yes."

You: "The key is magic. It makes the van move."

Your Kid: "Wow! What if you accidentally tried it on the house?"

You: "You have to be careful, that's for sure!"

Rule #2- Sacrifice Everything. Well, not really SACRIFICE, maybe more of a TRADE. As a Dad, get ready to trade reading the newspaper for 'Arthur's Underwear'; 'Seinfeld' for 'Dora the Explorer' and your plans to buy a new set of speakers for a booster seat and crib. The irony here is that when your kids get old enough, they will actually mock you over the fact that you no longer own ANY COOL STUFF. What you did have when you started out as a family has long since been busted, coloured on or thrown up into. The key here is to bide your time patiently until YOUR kids start reproducing, THEN go on a buying spree for all the stuff you've always wanted. Spend thousands. You'll love the looks on their faces.

Rule #3- Love Recklessly. I'm not just talking about your future wife here, either. Let your kids know every day that YOU LOVE THEM. This means that you must tell them. With your mouth. Even when you want nothing more than to send them far, far away from you for a very long time. Now I know that guys aren't the best "communicators" in the world. They don't have to be. These are kids we're talking about. They have nothing to compare your skills as a father. A passing grade here is a great big hug, out of the blue from junior. Plus, when they are teenagers, you can REALLY mess them up by proclaiming your love for them in a variety of places, not least of which is the local mall. "But I've always told you that I loved you..." will be your best defense.

Remember, son, Fatherhood is the greatest sport of all. It goes for twenty four hours a day, seven days a week. It fills you with despair, fatigue and frustration. But there is no other sport that can lift you to the heights of pride and exhilaration; no other task that promises the rich return that Fatherhood does.

Someday, I hope you will say "I want to be just like you." Then I'll know that I won.

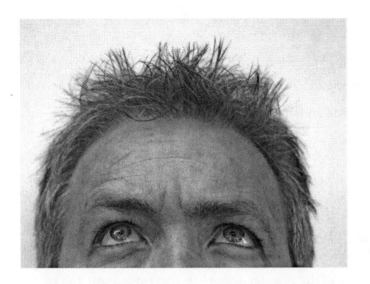

Financial Planners

the reason that most people (and by most people, I mean me) don't go to a Financial Planner is because they (the people) don't want them (the Planners) to know that they (the people or the Planners) have the financial sense of a carrot. Financial Planners are quite aware of this. In fact, it's a big joke at Financial Planner coffee shops and Tupperware parties, how easy it is to mess normal people up. That is why, when you finally give in to your wife's pleas and make The Appointment, you must prepare yourself both mentally and emotionally. The Planner will sit back in his leather chair and ask you pertinent investment questions such as: "So, how much money do you intend to spend on pets when you are over the age of seventy?" and "How many years do you think your three and five year old will spend in post-secondary education?" Now, the problem is that, even if you know the answer and you tell him, he will ask you ANOTHER, even MORE detailed question.

212

You: "We know now that our five year old will attend university for four years and get his degree in Biophysics and our three year old will get her Master's in Civil Aviation Mechanics."

Financial Planner: "Turbo-prop or jet engine?"

You: "Uuh...we're not sure."

Financial Planner: "What kind of parents are you, anyways?"

The favorite trick of the Planner, though, is that even though YOU are paying HIM, he gets to give you HOMEWORK.

Financial Planner: "Okay, I need to get a really good picture of your financial situation so I'll get you to fill out this three page question-naire detailing every dollar you've paid out to anyone in the last three hundred and sixty-five days. Heaven help you if you are not completely accurate."

But do not think for one minute that it is all hardship and bad news. I can tell you for a fact that once we had figured out exactly how much we spent on phone bills, clothing, personal care, public transportation and wall paintings (oil and/or watercolor),we were able to get a fairly accurate report about where we stood.

Financial Planner: "Well, by looking at everything you've supplied for me, I've been able to determine that, after all your bills and debts were taken care of last year, you had a surplus of fifteen thousand dollars."

★★★★SILENCE★★★★

Financial Planner: "Ahem...as I said, you had a surplus of fifteen thousand dollars. Do either of you know where that is right now?"

Me: "I, um, think that SHE has it."

My Wife: "What?"

Me: "Well, YOU handle all the money."

Financial Planner: "Ok, ok, actually everybody usually ends up with a surplus. That's just a little joke we play on people. Mark, I did find out that you have $53,000 of contribution room left in your RRSP."

Me: "Yeah. I, uh, didn't want to crowd it, you know, stuff it all in at one time..."

Financial Planner: "Well, that's a good plan, I guess...As we can see from my colored bar graph here, you'll be spending about $90,000 a year when you retire."

Me: "Cool!"

Financial Planner: "I don't think you understand. Where will that money come from?"

Me: "Can we use the fifteen thousand dollars from last year?

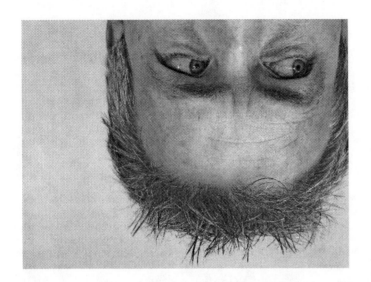

Hooked On Fishing

most women do not understand the art of fishing. To them, it is just an excuse for a bunch of guys to get together in a boat for extended periods of time, eating, drinking and breaking wind. Strangely, even though this is their opinion, they still let their husbands go. "Better out on the lake than in my basement," is basically what the average Canadian wife is saying.

Now I know what you are thinking. You are thinking: "What about me, Mark? How can I become a fisherman?" Luckily for you I couldn't think of a GOOD topic to write about this week, so I will use this space to help you get started.

Before you do anything, you must purchase a fishing licence. In Ontario, we pay about twelve bucks a year for the right to fish in our beautiful lakes, rivers, creeks and ditches. We all know, deep down in our hearts, that there aren't actually any fish in these bodies of water. That does not deter us from leaving the family for days at a time and pretending. And the money that is collected from all the sportsmen all over the province every year goes directly into putting more fish that don't exist into the water.

Once the legal side is taken care of, there is much equipment to gather. You need a reel (the thing that holds the fishing line), a rod (the long, flexible stick that holds the reel), a tackle box (a fisherman's tool box that contains lures, hooks, bobbers and WD-40), a friend with a boat and a cooler ('nuff said).

You can take it from me, an old fishing pro, it doesn't matter what type of equipment you buy, it all does the same job. Many rookies walk into a store and get tricked into spending a huge wad of dough on the stuff that has all the fancy bells and whistles, only to find that it works the same as anything else on the shelf. It's embarrassing how easily some people are fooled!

It takes an experienced eye to be able to walk into a sportsmen's store, sift through all the flashy clap-trap and grab the things that a good fisherman can REALLY use without getting ripped off. Like, for instance, an item I found on the way up to the cottage, called POWERBAIT. This is bait for fish that you can purchase in the more discerning stores that is SYNTHETICALLY CREATED to drive all fish wild. You can tell by the name it is not fake. Plus, it is packaged in GOLD FOIL. This alerts the discerning fisherman to the fact that these guys will spare no expense when it comes to the preparation and packaging of their fine product.

And one whiff of the item in question will erase any doubt as to its effectiveness under water. In fact, the fish in question could be floating ON TOP of the water and they would still smell this bait. "Turns fishes' heads while turning your stomach" should be its motto. Of course, as a consummate professional, I have further customised this already 'bold' lure. By that I mean that I left it in my tackle box in the hot sun for a solid week, further strengthening the powerful allure of this bait to a level 10-(Halibut hockey bag).

I want you to know that even though my instincts told me this was the product to purchase, I still peppered the vendor with questions:

Me: "So, does this POWERBAIT in the gold foil package work?"

Vendor: "So far."

Me: "What kind of fish does it attract?"

Vendor: "Oh, the usual kind. Large mouths, Wide eyes and Suckers."

Me: "Wow. Sounds like I'm in luck."

Vendor: "I know I'm happy with it!"

And there you have it. I'm sure, had there actually been any fish in the lake, they would have been driven wild.

ABOUT THE AUTHOR

Who is this mysterious Mark Thrice and why has he never been seen at the same time as millionaire playboy John Hollingsworth…or for that matter, Donald Trump?

The truth is that John Hollingsworth and Mark Thrice are the same person! The details are a little sketchy right now. (There may have been an operation in Sweden.) But suffice it to say that Mr. Hollingsworth has been quietly building his empire out of Sarnia, Ontario, Canada.

When he is not writing his syndicated humor column, he is a highly sought-after speaker and entertainer who uses his expertise as an improv comic to deliver powerful…and powerfully questionable presentations.

John, Mark, their wife Stephanie and three children live in a cozy house in Sarnia with two guinea pigs that are not long for this world.

Printed in the United States
97934LV00003B/46-78/A